T0295670

Small Business, Big Government and the Origins of Enterprise Policy

The Report of the Committee of Inquiry on Small Firms (the Bolton Committee Report) was produced at a time of significant political change. The 1970s in the UK saw the beginning of the end for interventionism and 'big government' and the emergence of a new free market, economic liberalism. However, the same period also saw the creation of what became a substantial agenda to intervene in the economy through an extensive range of government initiatives aimed at encouraging and enabling small firms and entrepreneurship.

Marking the 50th Anniversary of the publication of the Bolton Committee's report, this book provides researchers with new insights into the tensions between these potentially contradictory political agendas that would come to shape our modern economy. It provides the first in-depth analysis of the origins, operation and outcomes of the Bolton Committee, which is widely seen as responsible for the small firm agenda in the UK. In doing so, new insights are generated not only into the birth of enterprise policy in the UK but also into the wider changes in political economy that saw powerful tensions between free-market rhetoric and new forms of interventionism in practice.

The book will be of interest to scholars and PhD students working in the fields of entrepreneurship, small business management and business history.

Robert Wapshott is Associate Professor in Entrepreneurship and Innovation at the Haydn Green Institute, University of Nottingham, UK.

Oliver Mallett is Professor of Entrepreneurship at the University of Stirling, UK.

Routledge Focus on Business and Management

The fields of business and management have grown exponentially as areas of research and education. This growth presents challenges for readers trying to keep up with the latest important insights. *Routledge Focus on Business and Management* presents small books on big topics and how they intersect with the world of business research.

Individually, each title in the series provides coverage of a key academic topic, whilst collectively, the series forms a comprehensive collection across the business disciplines.

Culture and Resilience at Work
A Study of Stress and Hardiness among Indian Corporate Professionals
Pallabi Mund

Optimal Spending on Cybersecurity Measures
Risk Management
Tara Kissoon

Small Business, Big Government and the Origins of Enterprise Policy
The UK Bolton Committee
Robert Wapshott and Oliver Mallett

Conflict, Power, and Organizational Change
Deborah A. Colwill

Human Resource Management for Organisational Change
Theoretical Formulations
Dr. Paritosh Mishra, Dr. Balvinder Shukla and Dr. R. Sujatha

For more information about this series, please visit: www.routledge.com/Routledge-Focus-on-Business-and-Management/book-series/FBM

Small Business, Big Government and the Origins of Enterprise Policy
The UK Bolton Committee

Robert Wapshott and Oliver Mallett

 Routledge
Taylor & Francis Group

NEW YORK AND LONDON

First published 2022
by Routledge
605 Third Avenue, New York, NY 10158

and by Routledge
2 Park Square, Milton Park, Abingdon, Oxon OX14 4RN

Routledge is an imprint of the Taylor & Francis Group, an informa business

© 2022 Robert Wapshott and Oliver Mallett

Library of Congress Cataloging-in-Publication Data
Names: Wapshott, Robert, author. | Mallett, Oliver, author.
Title: Small business, big government and the origins of enterprise policy:
the UK bolton committee / Robert Wapshott and Oliver Mallett.
Description: New York, NY : Routledge, 2022. |
Series: Routledge focus on business and management |
Includes bibliographical references and index.
Identifiers: LCCN 2021021387 (print) | LCCN 2021021388 (ebook) |
ISBN 9780367634308 (hbk) | ISBN 9780367634322 (pbk) |
ISBN 9781003119142 (ebk)
Subjects: LCSH: Small business–Great Britain. | Industrial policy–Great Britain. |
Industrial management–Great Britain. | Committees–Great Britain.
Classification: LCC HD2346.G7 W28 2022 (print) |
LCC HD2346.G7 (ebook) | DDC 338.6/420941–dc23
LC record available at https://lccn.loc.gov/2021021387
LC ebook record available at https://lccn.loc.gov/2021021388

ISBN: 978-0-367-63430-8 (hbk)
ISBN: 978-0-367-63432-2 (pbk)
ISBN: 978-1-003-11914-2 (ebk)

DOI: 10.4324/9781003119142

Typeset in Times New Roman
by Newgen Publishing UK

Contents

Acknowledgements

Robert Wapshott would like to acknowledge the support of the University of Sheffield, where the majority of his contribution to this work was completed, as well as the University of Nottingham and the Haydn Green Institute.

Oliver Mallett would like to acknowledge the support of the University of Stirling, as well as the previous support of Newcastle University. He would especially like to thank Rebecca, Lacey and Lola for all their love and support.

Both authors would like to thank colleagues at the Institute for Small Business and Entrepreneurship annual conference; the expert staff at the National Archives at Kew, London, and at the British Library (London and Boston Spa); and the reviewers of the proposal for this short-form book.

1 Small Business and Big Government

Introduction

In March 2021, the UK's Conservative Chancellor of the Exchequer, Rishi Sunak, set out a Budget for the national economy's post-COVID recovery. The Chancellor's plans sought to stimulate economic growth in an economy suffering from nearly 12 months of lockdowns and related restrictions. The Budget included significant funds in support of those with jobs threatened by the measures taken to address the pandemic, including a Self-Employment Income Support Scheme, together with Restart Grants, Recovery Loans and business rate relief.

New schemes were also launched to 'help small and medium sized businesses across the UK learn new skills, reach new customers and boost profits' (Help to Grow, 2021). The schemes, funded to over £500 million, offer heavily subsidised (90%) management training to 30,000 small and medium sized enterprises (SMEs) over three years and support for digital technology adoption via free advice and discounts on software. The 'Help to Grow' programmes represent examples of government action reflecting the importance attributed to SMEs for economic growth. While many of these measures are specific to a COVID response strategy, the general principle of government taking up a role in relation to what we can broadly consider 'enterprise' is not new.

Policies to support small firms and encourage entrepreneurship have been a consistent feature of political pledges from all mainstream UK parties since the 1970s (Wapshott and Mallett, 2018). In this book we are interested in how this political consensus on the role of government in relation to enterprise came about. How did the apparent consensus concerning the role of government acting to support private businesses through providing finance, subsidised business consultancy and advice or tax relief come about? Although such consensus today means there is little vocal dissent over these interventions, it is apparent that the

DOI: 10.4324/9781003119142-1

case for governments taking an active role in respect of SMEs in the economy has not always been so readily accepted.

Enterprise Policy

Internationally, there is significant government focus on small businesses and entrepreneurship that has involved a 'profound shift' in industrial policy and the relationship between politics and business, involving a pivot away from managed economies to entrepreneurial economies (Gilbert et al., 2004). Interestingly, in the UK, this interventionist approach emerged as the era of the 'planned economy' was coming to an end and a new era of free markets and small government was loudly hailed as the future. During the 1970s, the UK appeared to usher in the beginning of the end for interventionism and industrial coordination by 'big government' as ideas of a new free market, economic liberalism gained influence. Under these developing ideas, the role of governments would change from a traditionally close involvement with the operation of industry to acting to facilitate a competitive and dynamic economy. In this new environment, enterprise policy, those government initiatives and interventions aimed at encouraging and enabling small firms and entrepreneurship in the economy, was to have an important role.

The shift towards enterprise policy has given rise to tensions within free market political systems as many governments following a 'small government', free market agenda simultaneously invest heavily in policies to support and promote new ventures and small businesses, including subsidised access to finance and consultancy services. In the UK this led a free market, Conservative government to create a business support service (Business Link) that was seen by some commentators as representing a nationalisation of small business support (Priest, 1999). The seemingly contradictory role of enterprise policy interventions within free market political systems, and their historical foundations in the development of UK enterprise policy, have received little attention.

The Committee of Inquiry on Small Firms

The Report of the Committee of Inquiry on Small Firms (1971) chaired by John Bolton, and widely known as the Bolton Committee, is 50 years old at our time of writing. The Committee's two years of work on the report was conducted at a time of political change and uncertainty, when small businesses and entrepreneurship were largely overlooked in political debates and the operations of government. It was a time in the UK when small businesses were commonly viewed as an industrial throwback set against the advances of large-scale industry (Galbraith, 1972). This position of small businesses, and their relation to government, at the time of the Bolton Committee was clearly very different from the position they find themselves in today when 'virtually all organs of government have programs which qualify as either EP [entrepreneurship policies] or SMEP [SME policies]' (Lundström et al., 2014, p.946). Such programmes and interventions come at a cost, in the UK this is estimated to have exceeded £8bn or even £12bn per year (Hughes, 2008; Richard, 2008).

The Bolton Committee Report marked a transition in how small firms were viewed and treated in the UK. Small firms moved from being overlooked in discussions of industrial policy to being represented by a Small Firms Division within the machinery of government. From industrial throwbacks, variously romanticised and disparaged, they came to be accepted as a sector bearing a mantle of economic dynamism and renewal that would subsequently attract support from each of the mainstream national political parties. This new agenda, embracing small firms, would prove highly influential for a refocusing of industrial policy on enterprise and entrepreneurship policy.

The Committee's report was welcomed in Parliament on 3 November 1971 as the 'first authoritative study of the place of the small firm in our economy' (HC Deb, 1971) and has been regarded as 'path-breaking' (Bennett, 2014, p.77) in three respects. Firstly, the Bolton Report brought consideration of small firms into mainstream discussions of economic growth, according them serious political attention (Bennett, 2011). Secondly, it shaped and entrenched the idea and definition of small firms in national political debate (Binks and Coyne, 1983). Thirdly, as 'a pioneering study of the role of small firms in the economy' (McHugh, 1979, p.46), it formed 'the bedrock of virtually all research, analysis and policy making' (Curran and Stanworth, 1982, p.3). As Blackburn and Smallbone (2008, p.276) highlight, 'From Bolton numerous lobby groups, research projects, academic research groups, and outlets for dissemination were spawned.'

The Formation of Enterprise Policies

Analysing the workings of the Bolton Committee casts new light on the complexities of enterprise policymaking processes. Authors such as Smallbone and Welter (2020) have highlighted the importance but also the challenges of studying these processes, the people involved and the influence of context. They emphasise the importance of differentiating between the four stages of the policy process: agenda setting, policy formulation, implementation and evaluation. Our analysis provides important insights into the first three of these stages.

Further, our approach provides access to the frequently obscured ways in which, as Arshed and Carter (2012) note, the development of enterprise policy does not follow prescribed processes. Arshed and Carter identify four key influences on the policymaking process, which we explore in this book: the legitimacy (internal, external and media) necessary to establish credibility; the behaviours of individual actors; shared norms and beliefs in departmental cultures; and political actors who overrule civil servants. In overcoming some of the difficulties of access and perspective that have limited previous studies of enterprise policymaking and the various factors that shape it, the historical analysis we present in this book provides a powerful lens on the enterprise policymaking process.

Despite the significance and wide citation of the Bolton Committee in studies of small firms in general and enterprise policy more specifically, it is seldom discussed in depth. Understanding this state of affairs might be explained, at least in part, by the idea that the emergence of an explicit enterprise policy agenda coincided with a retreat by business historians from widespread engagement with entrepreneurship. Wadhwani and Lubinski, (2017) argue that 'it was exactly when historians were moving away from entrepreneurship as a major area of research' that entrepreneurship was coming to provide 'the framing language with which business people and policymakers describe what drives markets and economies' (2017, p.773). As such, despite the importance attached to the Bolton Committee's report, the operation of the Committee itself has gone largely unexamined bar a handful of texts.

As part of their broader consideration of *The Political Economy of the Small Firm*, Dannreuther and Perren (2013) detail some of the politics involved in setting up the Committee and its subsequent influence in political debate. Further, Thomson's (2016) biography of John Bolton provides insights into the Committee and its impact through a biography of the Committee's Chair. However, both contributions engage with the Committee's work as part of their wider respective projects, leaving opportunities for further exploration of how the Committee's ongoing work was shaped by its turbulent political context to provide new insights into this historical moment and into enterprise policymaking processes more generally.

References back to the significance of the Bolton Report by scholars and politicians are typically disconnected from analysis of how the Committee was formed in an era dominated by large businesses, how the voices of small businesses and entrepreneurs were represented or how the influence of wider political debates about the role of government in the economy and industry came to bear on its deliberations. Given the significance of the conclusions reached by the Committee and their subsequent influence, it is important to understand the processes by which these conclusions were reached and the context that shaped these processes.

Understanding the Context for UK Policymaking

The necessity to study things in their context is well recognised in the field of entrepreneurship. Engaging with context requires that events are analysed in light of, among other things, temporal, historical and institutional factors (Welter, 2011). Adhering to this view and engaging with an established body of work by scholars of politics and policymaking, our work is informed by an historical institutionalist perspective that is concerned with how policies and policy agendas develop in relation to institutions. Pierson (1996, p.126) argues that political development takes place over time and that 'many of the contemporary implications of these temporal processes are embedded in institutions'. An historical institutionalist perspective holds value for studying politics and policymaking in the field of SMEs and entrepreneurship because it helps us recognise that deliberations and recommendations reflect not only the views of the day but also the underlying, pre-existing structures at work *and* that decisions taken at one time can continue to shape outcomes, in one way or another, long into the future.

Further establishing the context for our study's focus, we have drawn on the work of Hall (1986) who sets out the four key structural aspects of the British state that provide an important context for understanding influences on policy and are of relevance to our study of the Bolton Committee's origins, development and production of a report and set of recommendations. The first is Britain's position within the international system which, in the 1960s, was a significant source of uncertainty and concern. There was an existential concern about the country's place in the world, a persistent sense of decline. Through the 1950s and 1960s it was clear that British manufacturing was in trouble. Manufacturing output and productivity was growing at a slower rate than competitor nations, exports were suffering and, as Matthews (2007, p.775) records, profitability was falling such that 'by the late 1970s profits in British manufacturing were perhaps approaching zero'. This represented a general sense of national and economic decline. The degree to which the country was in decline is disputed and a debate outside the scope of this book. However, the worries were real and were exacerbated by concerns about Sterling and around the balance of payments.

The second important factor is society's organisational configuration which can affect the problems faced and the capacity to deal with them, such as the influence of the trade unions, which at this time were a dominant political influence, both through the Labour Party and other key political institutions. Of particular importance for our focus was the organisational configuration necessitated by a tripartite means of negotiation between the state, industry and workers. This can be clearly seen in the influence of the National Economic Development Council, which we discuss in detail in Chapter 3.

The third factor Hall emphasises is the institutional structure of the state itself, affecting 'the set of incentives, balance of power, and flow of information facing individuals at different positions within it [and therefore] the kind of policies they are likely to implement' (p.282). Key institutions such as the Bank of England and HM Treasury exert considerable influence on UK policymaking processes and what is seen as viable (or not). As we will see repeatedly in the analysis that follows, the fact that the Treasury needs to provide the funds for large-scale policy initiatives gives it a huge influence, not only in terms of the initial establishment of the Bolton Committee but also on its development and the recommendations it produced.

Fourthly, it is also important to understand the nature of the wider political system, which can be interpreted as a network of political parties and interest intermediaries that seek to influence policy. For example, Hall notes the need to go through political parties and their ties to particular interest groups for 'finance, advice and personnel' (p.286). We discuss the political context in detail in Chapter 6 but the role of the main political parties and interest groups acting as intermediaries are a key part of understanding the position of small firms and their interests at this time. As we will see throughout the book, each of the factors Hall identifies shape what government and policymakers see as possible, how policies develop and, importantly, how they are implemented.

How We Studied the Committee's Work

To examine the formation, operations and outputs of the Bolton Committee, we analysed materials held in open files at the UK's National Archives at Kew in London. We examined records from the Committee and associated files along with published contemporary materials accessed via the British Library and other subsequent publications. We therefore present an account of the Committee that draws on a wide range of the sources and documents associated with the Committee and its work. The sources drawn on directly in this text are referenced accordingly, while sources more widely from the Board of Trade, the Treasury and other interested departments have been reviewed in developing our account of the Committee. We are very grateful to the staff at the National Archives for their assistance in our research. Our thanks are also offered to the staff at the British Library in Boston Spa, especially when working under the various restrictions of COVID-19.

In studying the workings of the Bolton Committee, we have drawn in detail on the Committee's meeting minutes which record the business of the Committee. Through the minutes we can get a sense of the planning of the Committee's work alongside members' recorded views on the task they faced, responses to evidence received and the discussions held. The archival records also feature submissions from interested stakeholder bodies and small business owners, presenting their perspective on government treatment of small firms. Moreover, there are records from the oral hearings contributing to the evidence base for the Committee, in addition to various news items commenting on small firms or the work of the Committee and the 18 research reports commissioned and published by the Committee. We engage with this evidence submitted to, and gathered by, the Committee in Chapters 4 and 5, including the large-scale survey exercise that was conducted.

Having access to these detailed records is important in allowing us to analyse in detail the processes by which influential documents such as the Bolton Committee's report are produced. Studies of enterprise policy have highlighted the need to research policymaking processes as well as analysing the finished policies and effects. Studying the contemporary documents facilitates the generation of insights, including into the early stages of the policy process and the forms of intervention, such as by elected politicians, that may not be available to researchers studying policymaking in the present day (Smallbone and Welter, 2020).

The Structure of the Book

In this book we set out to analyse the rise of small firms through our study of the Bolton Committee. We detail how small firms were brought in from the political wilderness, the extensive research effort undertaken by the Committee and how the Committee navigated the transforming political environment of the late 1960s and early 1970s. This analysis is placed within the shifting context of the times. In doing so, we demonstrate new insights not only into the birth of enterprise policy in the UK but also into the wider changes in political economy that saw powerful tensions between free market rhetoric and new forms of interventionism that were developing in practice. To do so, the book adopts the following structure:

Chapter 2, *The small firm in the age of the giant enterprise*, outlines the historical background to the creation of the Bolton Committee. It traces the decline in political significance of small firms, as national priorities turned towards large-scale enterprises, economies of scale and international competition.

Chapter 3, *From little acorns: The origins and establishment of the Bolton Committee*, outlines the origins of the Bolton Committee. Setting the Committee's roots in the major political debates of the era, the chapter draws out the role of key stakeholder organisations in moves to establish an inquiry into the problems facing small firms, leading to the agreed terms of reference.

Chapter 4, *Searching for answers: Listening to small firms and other stakeholders*, provides insights to the data collection undertaken by the Committee and the challenges encountered in its analysis. The chapter examines the findings from the Committee's postal survey as well as examining submissions made to the Committee.

Chapter 5, *Searching for answers: The Committee's data collection effort*, concentrates on the detailed research undertaken in the research reports commissioned by the Committee. The reports cover interesting areas including industry-specific analyses of small firms and analyses of small firms in the economy, as well as highlighting some of the challenges associated with researching small firms at the time.

Chapter 6, *Small business and small government?*, emphasises the political changes occurring during the two-year period in which the Committee completed its work. Established under a Labour government, the Committee would complete its report under Heath's Conservative government, which had set out changes in the scope of government and in government's relationship with industry.

Chapter 7, *Recommending the future of enterprise policy: A less than dramatic response*, discusses the report's recommendations and how these were received in government and more widely. The chapter concludes with an overview of the reactions to the report from politicians, civil servants, small business groups and the Business Press.

Chapter 8, *Bolton 50 years on*, concludes this book by discussing the influence of the Report and its recommendations and the significance of the Committee's work as the largest study of small firms conducted in the UK at that time and since. The chapter traces how the work of the Committee represents an important period of transition and contradictions in the development of enterprise policy, leading up to Thatcher's enterprise culture.

References

Arshed, N. and Carter, S. (2012). Enterprise policymaking in the UK: Prescribed approaches and day-to-day practice. In: R.A. Blackburn and M.T. Schaper (eds.) *Government, SMEs and entrepreneurship development: Policy, practice and challenges.* Farnham: Gower, pp.61–74.

Bennett, R. (2011). *Local business voice: The history of Chambers of Commerce in Britain, Ireland, and revolutionary America 1760–2011.* Oxford: Oxford University Press.

Bennett, R. (2014). *Entrepreneurship, small business and public policy: Evolution and revolution.* Abingdon: Routledge.

Binks, M. and Coyne, J. (1983). *The birth of enterprise: An analytical and empirical study of the growth of small firms.* London: The Institute of Economic Affairs.

Blackburn, R.A. and Smallbone, D. (2008). Researching small firms and entrepreneurship in the UK: Developments and distinctiveness. *Entrepreneurship Theory and Practice*, 32(2), 267–288.

Bolton, J.E. (1971). *Committee of inquiry on small firms,* Cmnd. 4811. London: H.M.S.O. (reprint).

Curran, J. and Stanworth, J. (1982). Bolton ten years on: A research inventory and critical review. In: J. Stanworth, A. Westrip, D. Watkins, and J. Lewis (eds.) *Perspectives on a decade of small business research: Bolton ten years on.* Gower: Aldershot, pp.3–27.

Dannreuther, C. and Perren, L. (2013). *The political economy of the small firm.* Abingdon: Routledge.

Galbraith, J.K. (1972). *The new industrial state* (2nd edition). Harmondsworth: Penguin Books.

Gilbert, B.A., Audretsch, D.B. and McDougall, P.P. (2004). The emergence of entrepreneurship policy. *Small Business Economics*, 22(3–4): 313–323.

Hall, P.A. (1986). The state and economic decline. In: B. Elbaum and W. Lazonick (eds.) *The decline of the British economy.* Oxford: Oxford University Press, pp.266–302.

HC Deb (1971). vol.825 col.188, John Davies, MP, 3 November.

Help to Grow (2021). URL: https://helptogrow.campaign.gov.uk/ Accessed 02.05.21.

Hughes, A. (2008). Entrepreneurship and innovation policy: Retrospect and prospect. *The Political Quarterly*, 79(s1): 133–152.

Lundström, A., Vikström, P., Fink, M., Meuleman, M., Głodek, P., Storey, D. and Kroksgård, A. (2014). Measuring the costs and coverage of SME and entrepreneurship policy: A pioneering study. *Entrepreneurship Theory & Practice*, 38(4): 941–957.

Matthews, D. (2007). The performance of British manufacturing in the Post-War long boom. *Business History*, 49(6): 763–779.

McHugh, J. (1979). The self-employed and the small independent entrepreneur. In: R. King and N. Nugent (eds.) *Respectable rebels*. London: Hodder and Stoughton, pp.46–75.

Pierson, P. (1996). The path to European integration a historical institutionalist analysis. *Comparative Political Studies*, 29(2): 123–163.

Priest, S.J. (1999). Business Link services to small and medium-sized enterprises: Targeting, innovation, and charging. *Environment and Planning C: Government and Policy*, 17(2): 177–194.

Richard, D. (2008). *Small business and government: The Richard report*. Available at: www.conservatives.com/pdf/document-richardreport-2008.pdf Accessed: 20.08.18.

Smallbone, D. and Welter, F. (2020). An introduction to a research agenda for entrepreneurship policy: Why we need a different agenda on entrepreneurship policy. In: D. Smallbone and F. Welter (eds.) *A research agenda for entrepreneurship policy*. Cheltenham: Edward Elgar, pp.1–14.

Thomson, A. (2016). *Small business, education and management: The life and times of John Bolton*. Abingdon: Routledge.

Wadhwani, R.D. and Lubinski, C. (2017). Reinventing entrepreneurial history. *Business History Review*, 91: 767–799.

Wapshott, R. and Mallett, O. (2018). Small and medium-sized enterprise policy: Designed to fail? *Environment and Planning C: Politics and Space*, 36(4): 750–772.

Welter, F. (2011). Contextualizing entrepreneurship—Conceptual challenges and ways forward. *Entrepreneurship Theory and Practice*, 35(1): 165–184.

2 The Small Firm in the Age of the Giant Enterprise

Introduction

While the Bolton Committee and its report marked an important shift in how small firms were viewed, and initiated activities that inform key elements of modern enterprise policy agendas, government policies targeting small firms had been in existence long before the Committee began its work. These policy initiatives were often disparate and relatively small in scale but they did seek to address small firm-specific concerns and acknowledged the importance of small firms for regional development. We have written in detail elsewhere about the historical development of enterprise policy in the UK (Mallett and Wapshott, 2020); our purpose here is to set out the position of small firms in the years prior to the Bolton Committee, during which the trend was of national priorities oriented towards large-scale enterprises, economies of scale and international competition. In this chapter we establish the background to the Bolton Committee in terms of how governments and politicians had tended to view small businesses in the UK, and the historical relationship between government and small businesses.

We begin by outlining the political environment in the UK for our period of interest. We then provide a brief overview of the 'pre-history' of UK enterprise policy, which involved localised relations between (local) government and small business without any recognisable enterprise policymaking. The situation changed with the intervention of the Macmillan Committee in 1931 which led to policies focused on supporting small firms' access to finance and placing an emphasis on their regional role in tackling unemployment. The chapter concludes with a discussion of the move towards 'industrial reorganisation' and a predominant government focus on the large businesses that had come to dominate the UK political and economic landscape.

DOI: 10.4324/9781003119142-2

Party Politics in the UK

The UK Parliament is made up of an elected chamber and a non-elected second chamber that, for our period of focus in this book, governed the nations of England, Northern Ireland, Scotland and Wales (UK Parliament, 2021). In this book we focus on UK politics and policies without attending to differences in Northern Ireland, Scotland or Wales that were largely outside the scope of the Bolton Committee's work. The House of Commons is populated with elected Members of Parliament (MPs) who represent geographical constituencies from across the UK. In 1970, there were 630 MPs sitting in the House of Commons. The second chamber of the UK Parliament is the House of Lords, a non-elected body that examines and revises bills (draft laws) from the Commons. For over 100 years, UK politics has been dominated by three UK-wide political parties: the Conservatives, Labour and the Liberals (currently the Liberal Democrats). These parties are best considered as loose groupings of interests and ideas not as closely knit, ideologically unified movements.

The Liberal Party descends from the historic Whigs, which had been protectionist, though the central uniting idea of the Liberal Party has been of free trade and often individualism. These ideas were popular with the industrial and commercial interests that had risen to greater prominence in the nineteenth century. While the Liberals had consistently been a party of government through the second half of the nineteenth century, in the primary period of interest for this book (1969–1971), they were barely represented in Parliament. In the 1966 General Election, the Liberals under Jo Grimond secured 2.3 million votes, of the 27.3 million votes cast, while in 1970, this time under the leadership of Jeremy Thorpe, the party received 2.1 million votes from a total of 28.3 million ballots cast. Nevertheless, given how seats are allocated, this resulted in only 12 seats and 6 seats respectively being held by the Liberal Party in the House of Commons (Craig, 1990). We therefore focus in this book on the Labour and Conservative parties whose agendas and political representatives had the greater interaction with the Bolton Committee as the party in government or providing the principal opposition.

The Conservative party emerged in its modern guise in the 1830s (Blake, 2012) and has historically been more closely associated with the landowning and wealthy middle classes. The Conservatives (also known as the Tories, the party that preceded the Conservatives back to the seventeenth century) had moved away from some elements of laissez-faire capitalism in the nineteenth century, including the recognition of trade unions and the introduction of new regulations for industry. However, in general it adopted 'the prevailing Victorian preference for curtailing government in favour of local autonomy and economy' (Pugh, 2002, p.60), albeit with some persistent protectionist tendencies. In the nineteenth century, politics was largely played out in terms of the Conservatives and the Liberals, with a party explicitly for the interests of labour not formed until the end of the century (leading to the modern Labour Party, discussed later in the chapter).

To understand the political and historical background to the work of the Bolton Committee, it is important for us to consider the place of small businesses in the policies that have emerged from this political system.

A Brief Pre-History of Enterprise Policy in the UK

The nineteenth-century UK economy was dominated by owner-managed small-scale enterprises. They were often locally based and operated in hypercompetitive markets. Nonetheless, levels of demand were so high that, even in industries dominated by large businesses, smaller enterprises still proliferated. For example, this period saw an increased number of small-scale shops in response to the demand from urban concentrations of the working class. These shops, in turn, relied upon extensive supply chains to fill their shelves, often including a variety of other small businesses.

Small businesses and entrepreneurs were well placed to exert political influence at a regional level, shaping important elements of their operating environment. They were traditionally local employers and figures of high status within communities. There was also an increasing variety of people within those 'middle classes' supported by business profits rather than wages. They were often locally focused and contributed significantly to the social, cultural and political life of their towns and cities (Nenadic, 1991). This impact included changes in patterns of consumption, the urban environment, the organisation of work and working lives. These changes created various forms of local influence, including politically. For example, the newly influential owner-managers in manufacturing were seen as 'the arbiters of social relationships with the factory workforce, a disproportionately important element of the working population' (ibid., p.80).

However, especially after the 1860s, there was increasing competitive pressure from larger businesses as they began to more effectively leverage economies of scale. Economic recession and a downward trend in prices increased the struggles and marginalisation faced by many small businesses. Large businesses replaced the small, family businesses that had traditionally existed, often through the 'absorption and competitive elimination' of small firms (Hannah, 1983, p.1). The creation of monopolies through mergers and acquisitions was not viewed by government as an area for intervention, despite calls for the protection of the individualism and free competition that some argued small firms represented. The political interests of these firms began to focus on more immediate financial concerns such as those around business rates, while the interests and focus of politicians were increasingly on the large firms rising to prominence.

The increasing influence of organised labour drew attention to the fact that the working class was not represented in Parliament. The Independent Labour Party (ILP) was formed in 1893, heavily shaped by socialist intellectuals, though resisting adoption of the 'socialist' label. This was followed by the Labour Representation Committee (LRC) in 1900, an organisation established to sponsor and support left wing, trade union and other working-class political candidates. It was the LRC that then became the Labour Party in 1906, with the ILP affiliated to it. The Labour Party was formed of those MPs within the earlier groups. Its key ideas were around central planning and nationalisation of industry and it was therefore focused on workers and industries, not on small firms. As we will see in the next chapter, the Labour Party would quickly grow in support and influence, especially with universal male suffrage in 1918.

Following the perceived success of economies of scale gained through new technologies and the national coordination of war and economic crises, the first half of the twentieth century witnessed significant changes in the relationship between government and industry. There were policies and support for small businesses and entrepreneurship, but these continued to be discrete, small scale, ad hoc activities addressing local problems, typically administered by local government (Beesley and Wilson, 1981). In contrast, war had necessitated the development of large-scale bureaucracy and regular consultation between central government and key non-governmental interests. The British Government's traditionally limited intervention in industry was replaced by a broad political consensus around intervention, the encouragement of mergers that saw small firms merge into large combines and, in some industries, nationalisation. The trend towards mergers applied not only to manufacturing but also to services. For example, while it was not apparent at the time, more recent analyses of the interwar years have demonstrated a cartelisation and a tendency for the large banks to confine their activities to the formal provision of short-term loans to largely captive markets, reaping monopoly profits (Scott and Newton, 2007). The implications of these changes in the financial sector for small businesses would come to form an important factor for the emergence of enterprise policy.

The First UK Enterprise Policies

The Macmillan Committee on Finance and Industry was set up in 1929 to 'inquire into banking, finance and credit [...] and to make recommendations calculated to enable these agencies to promote the development of trade and commerce and the employment of labour' (Macmillan, 1931, p.vi). The National Chamber of Trade represented small businesses' concerns to the Committee that they were significantly challenged in accessing finance for industrial growth. The Committee's report did not engage with these claims in any detail (or seek to corroborate them through additional evidence) but it did draw attention to the concerns. What would become known as the 'Macmillan Gap' in financing for small businesses produced an object of enterprise policy and a key path for enterprise policymaking, attempting to fix supply-side problems in small firm access to finance. This took the form of initiatives such as Credit for Industry and the Industrial and Commercial Finance Corporation (see Mallett and Wapshott, 2020).

The identification of the Macmillan gap and its potential implications for economic growth led to the development of a regional policy focus in early enterprise policies. For example, the 1934 Special Areas Act included a £1 million loan fund targeted at supporting small enterprises in areas of high unemployment. New trading estates were also established in the Special Areas. These estates were very large, publicly visible areas of dedicated industrial land where factories were built and rented to businesses by non-profit-making government-financed companies. The estates included research and sales staff to provide advice for tenants, for example on markets and sales methods in addition to other consultancy services (Scott, 2000).

These early enterprise policies established core areas of future enterprise policy initiatives, but they remained 'pitifully small' in their scope (Rubinstein, 2003, p.190) and were described by Labour politician Aneurin Bevan as 'an idle and empty farce' (cited in Stevenson and Cook, 1994, p.76). For example, fewer than 50,000 new jobs were created under the Special Areas legislation. On such limited scale, the schemes were never going to redress the regional disparities and huge levels of unemployment and deprivation experienced in the UK during the 1930s.

Industrial Reorganisation

For government during the interwar years, politicians across the spectrum had come to believe in (or at least espouse) the importance of 'rationalisation' and 'industrial reorganisation' (Greaves, 2017). This agenda sought improvements in technological advances, management structures and on the 'optimal' size of businesses to achieve increased productivity and economic growth. 'Optimal size' meant large firms created through mergers, processes supported by government (e.g. by removing perceived barriers), in search of efficiency and with a belief in the benefits of economies of scale.

Following World War II and the election of a Labour government, industrial policy saw a significant shift in the boundary between public and private economic activities. Millward and Singleton (2002, p.309) explain that by the end of the 1940s, '... half of annual capital expenditure in the UK was undertaken in the public sector of which some 40 per cent was accounted for by the nationalised industries'. An agenda developed around social democracy, broadly Keynesian interventionist policies, a mixed economy, the welfare state and full employment, continuing the trend of government focus on large businesses and leading Schumpeter (1949/2010, p.371) to '... infer that the principle of free enterprise' was no longer a strongly held view in the nation.

This was the period of embedded liberalism, where governments sought free trade but simultaneously provided welfare and sought to limit unemployment and avoid a repeat of the depression of the 1930s. In the UK, the post-war Labour government had been relatively successful in keeping unemployment low (and supporting those who were unemployed), and changes such as the National Health Service were to become a central part of national identity and pride for generations to come. When, following the 1951 election, Winston Churchill and the Conservatives returned to power, Labour had significantly remade the country. The Conservatives stayed in power until 1964 yet, broadly speaking, they reinforced a post-war consensus in continuing macroeconomic interventionism with no concerted effort to reverse the majority of what Labour had achieved. They were unprepared to risk a return to high levels of unemployment amidst outstanding national debt, the Korean War and the threat of balance of trade deficits. The Conservatives denationalised not only iron and steel, but also pursued areas of what can be considered new forms of nationalisation, for example with the creation with the UK Atomic Energy Commission.

In this age of the giant enterprise, conditions were difficult for small firms; an inability to access credit led many businesses to fail and the impacts were reported to the Bank of England by banks. Carnevali and Scott's (1999) archival research reveals that these effects were deliberately kept from being made public and that there 'is no mention in Bank of England files of possible measures that could be taken to avoid the credit restrictions forcing small firms into liquidation' (p.60). This demonstrates the significant limitations of early enterprise policy initiatives. It reflects a view at the time that small firms were a thing of the past, a dinosaur ill-equipped for the modern world. Indeed, writing on the industrial system, Galbraith (1972, pp.50–51) argued that 'By all but the pathologically romantic, it is now recognized that this is not the age of the small man'. Galbraith went further, setting out why the small firm was a thing of the past and explaining that the fortunes of small firms would not be revived by weakening larger firms. Rather, interventions to restore small firms would involve backward steps. It would mean engaging in processes of undoing much of what had been generally regarded as progress over the preceding 50 years. Where views such as this prevailed and political focus was on the opportunities of new technologies, new industries and the giant firm, enterprise policy in support of small firms could appear equally anachronistic.

Conclusion

In this chapter we have briefly outlined the historical background to our analysis of government and enterprise up to the late 1960s, the context for the work of the Bolton Committee. Changes in the political and economic landscape carried implications for small businesses as the era of small business and entrepreneurship (Bennett et al., 2020) was superseded by an age of large-scale enterprises in which government played a greater role in matters of industry. Against this backdrop, therefore, and for much of the twentieth century leading up to the Bolton Committee, small businesses attracted little political attention and there was only limited focus placed on these small businesses in terms of policy. What interventions and initiatives that did exist tended to be discrete, limited in scope and local in nature.

With changes in the economy and how government related to industry, small businesses appear to have been ineffective at making their voices heard. Rather, the position of small businesses was explained by others, perhaps most colourfully Galbraith, as large ventures became the focus of government attention. Despite this relative decline in status being observed by small business owners (Middlemas, 1986, 1990), there appear to have been few effective mechanisms for making their voices heard. As we shall see in Chapter 3, however, it would not be long before small businesses were climbing back up the political agenda.

References

Beesley, M.E. and Wilson, P.E.B. (1981). Government aid to small firms in Britain. In: P. Gorb, P. Dowell and P. Wilson (eds.) *Small business perspectives*. London: Armstrong Publishing/London Business School, pp.254–308.

Bennett, R., Smith, H., van Lieshout, C., Montebruno, P. and Newton, G. (2020). *The age of entrepreneurship: Business proprietors, self-employment and corporations since 1851*. Abingdon: Routledge.

Blake, R. (2012). *The Conservative Party from Peel to Major*. London: Faber & Faber.

Carnevali, F. and Scott, P. (1999). The Treasury as a venture capitalist: DATAC industrial finance and the Macmillan gap, 1945–60. *Financial History Review*, 6(1): 47–65.

Craig, F.W.S. (1990). *British General Election manifestos 1959–1987* (3rd edition). Aldershot: Parliamentary Research Services, Dartmouth (publisher).

Galbraith, J.K. (1972). *The new industrial state* (2nd edition). Harmondsworth: Penguin Books.

Greaves, J. (2017). *Industrial reorganization and government policy in interwar Britain*. Abingdon: Routledge.

Hannah, L. (1983). *The rise of the corporate economy* (2nd, revised edition). London: Methuen.

Macmillan, H. (1931). *Committee on Finance & Industry*. Report/Presented to Parliament by the Financial Secretary to the Treasury June 1931, Cmnd. 3897, London: H.M.S.O.

Mallett, O. and Wapshott, R. (2020). *A history of enterprise policy: Government, small business and entrepreneurship*. New York: Routledge.

Middlemas, K. (1986). *Power, competition and the state (Vol. 1) Britain in search of balance, 1940–1961*. London: The Macmillan Press.

Middlemas, K. (1990) *Power, competition and the state, volume 2: Threats to the postwar settlement: Britain, 1961–74*. Houndmills: Macmillan.

Millward, R. and Singleton, J. (2002). The ownership of British industry in the post-war era: An explanation. In: R. Millward and J. Singleton (eds.) *The political economy of nationalisation in Britain, 1920–1950*. Cambridge: Cambridge University Press, pp.309–320.

Nenadic, S. (1991). Businessmen, the urban middle classes, and the 'dominance' of manufacturers in nineteenth-century Britain. *Economic History Review*, 44(1): 66–85.

Pugh, M. (2002). *The making of modern British politics 1867–1945* (3rd edition). Oxford: Wiley-Blackwell.

Rubinstein, W.D. (2003). *Twentieth-century Britain: A political history.* Basingstoke: Palgrave Macmillan.

Schumpeter, J.A. (1949/2010). *Capitalism, socialism and democracy.* Abingdon: Routledge.

Scott, P. (2000). The audit of regional policy: 1934–1939. *Regional Studies,* 34(1): 55–65.

Scott, P. and Newton, N. (2007). Jealous monopolists? British banks and responses to the Macmillan gap during the 1930s. *Enterprise & Society,* 8(4): 881–919.

Stevenson, J. and Cook, C. (1994). *Britain in the depression: Society and politics, 1929–1939.* London: Longman.

UK Parliament (2021). UK Parliament, 2021, *Parliamentary website.* URL: www.parliament.uk/business/ Accessed: 04.07.21.

3 From Little Acorns

The Origins and Establishment of the Bolton Committee

Introduction

In this chapter we set out some of the context crucial to understanding the establishment and workings of the Bolton Committee. We begin by providing a brief overview of the social, economic and political context of the 1960s. We focus in particular on the National Economic Development Council (NEDC) and the tripartite means of industrial organisation and negotiation that was so important in the UK at this time.

It was from within the political framework of the NEDC that calls for a committee of inquiry into the position of small firms in the UK gained focus and credibility, specifically from the Confederation of British Industry (CBI). We outline the different voices involved in lobbying for small firms' interests at this time and the processes by which the Bolton Committee came to be established. We conclude the chapter by outlining the final makeup of the Committee itself and its terms of reference.

The Sixties in the UK

The UK is famous for the 'Swinging Sixties', a time of tumultuous social and cultural change. This decade saw a new youth culture emerge, famously including Beatlemania, and concluding, in 1969, with the release of David Bowie's 'Space Oddity'. Cultural changes, combined with reduced international power and influence associated with the gradual loss of empire, created not only uncertainties but also the space for potential new senses of national identity to emerge. Student protests, for example, attracted prominent attention in 1968, capturing some of the generational divide that resonated across Europe. However, for many small business owners, the technicolour pop of the 1960s did not

DOI: 10.4324/9781003119142-3

represent their day-to-day lives, emphasising some of the tensions emerging in a period of such significant cultural change (Fielding, 2003). The UK labour force had begun to undergo significant change. Throughout the 1950s and 1960s, there had been a shift away from manufacturing as services grew in prominence and represented a large part of the economy, although not yet as the major export that they would later become. Immigration had increased significantly as people from Commonwealth countries, such as those from Caribbean countries known as the 'Windrush Generation', were encouraged to migrate to the UK to address labour shortages and rebuild the economy after the Second World War. There were other changes as more women began to work outside the home, generally in low paid non-manual occupations. One in sixteen women were found by a government study to be self-employed, working particularly long hours and experiencing economic instability (LAB 8/3369). This period of change had significant political consequences.

The Political Context of Late Sixties Britain

The 1960s followed a period of relative stability and growing prosperity. In 1957, Conservative Prime Minister Harold Macmillan told his party that:

> Indeed let us be frank about it – most of our people have never had it so good. Go around the country, go to the industrial towns, go to the farms and you will see a state of prosperity such as we have never had in my lifetime – nor indeed in the history of this country.
>
> (BBC News, 1957)

Nonetheless, at the time of the Bolton Committee's formation, it was not the Conservatives but the Labour Party that formed the country's government. They came to power in 1964 following 13 years of Conservative governments. Irrespective of Macmillan's claims of success in improving living standards, Dunleavy (1989, p.265) describes how the 'erratic quality' of British macroeconomic policy meant that, despite high rates of growth in productivity and exports, there was a lack of a clear, agreed-upon direction of development for the economy. As Caines (2017, p.7) identifies, the Conservative governments that dominated the 1950s and 1960s failed to recognise how 'absolute growth and relative decline can and do co-exist and that they were contributing to the prolongation of a trend'.

The Labour Party, as with other political groups of the time, had utilised the narrative of national decline while in opposition to criticise the agenda of the government (Tomlinson, 2016). In its manifesto for the 1964 General Election campaign ('Let's go with Labour for the new Britain'), the Labour Party targeted the Conservatives' stop-go economic policy (Butler, 1995) such that 'Every jerk of expansion has ground to a full stop as the Government jams on the brake in a desperate attempt to combat inflation and rising prices.' In what it presented as a sharp contrast to the Conservatives' position, the Labour Party pledged to work with both industry and labour representatives to modernise the economy through a national economic plan.

At the polls in October 1964, the Labour Party was returned with a majority of four seats in the House of Commons (Labour: 317, Conservative: 304, Liberal: 9, Others: 0; Craig, 1990). Seeking a stronger majority, the Labour Prime Minister, Harold Wilson, called voters back to the polls in 1966 (Butler, 1995). The Labour government retained office with a landslide victory, providing an overall majority of 98 seats in the Commons (Labour: 364, Conservative: 253, Liberal: 12, Others: 1; Craig, 1990).

Harold Wilson had made his name in opposing the Labour Party's previous leadership (e.g. on cuts to social spending) and was more of a pragmatist than a politician aligned with a specific ideology. In the mid-1960s, Wilson was viewed in some quarters as a British John F. Kennedy (Kavanagh and Riches, 2016). He was perceived to have modernised and to some extent reinvigorated the Labour Party, in part by linking government planning to scientific and technological innovation to achieve economic growth. He also had his photo taken with the Beatles, something future leaders such as Tony Blair would seek to emulate with the pop stars of their day. The Beatles were also awarded MBEs ('Member of the Order of the British Empire') for their 'services to the export economy'. This award captures some of the tensions of the time, in bringing together popular culture, empire and the worries about the economy and the balance of payments.

While the Labour Party remained formally wedded to nationalisation and its foundation in the trade union movement, it contained a broad spectrum of political views. It had moved towards an 'industrial modernisation' agenda that was, at least in part, seen as a viable critique of the Conservatives' failures in producing sufficient economic growth. However, it also drew on ideas discussed within the Conservative Party from the late 1950s and continued to represent something of 'a cross-party (partial) consensus' (Tomlinson, 2004, p.7).

Influential figures in shaping the new agenda included Anthony Crosland, a prominent figure within the 'Gaitskellite' side of the Labour Party that represented this consensus (Kavanagh and Riches, 2016). Having served in government as Minister of State for Economic Affairs (1964–1965) and Secretary of State for Education and Science (1965–1967), Crosland was appointed as President of the Board of Trade between 1967 and 1969 (Who's Who, 2007). In 1956, he had published *The Future of Socialism*, which argued for a form of social democracy in the context of broad political consensus positioned from the right wing of the party (later editions featured a preface by Labour Chancellor of the Exchequer and future Prime Minister Gordon Brown and were subtitled 'The Book That Changed British Politics'). Crosland argued for a move away from the focus on ownership of the means of production and the importance of individual liberty and equality, with a vital role for contemporary, *progressive* capitalism and identifying the value of the *innovating entrepreneur*. This retained an important welfare state with government investment and a Keynesian economic approach.

However, while members of the new Wilson Government such as Crosland had talked up competition, 'When Labour came to power in 1964, pro-competition views were little in evidence, and throughout the next six years other issues were centre stage in industrial policy' (Tomlinson, 2004, p.113). As the government faced multiple crises, often stemming from external factors, concern was less focused on areas such as monopolies and more on worries that large firms had become lethargic, and again shaped by the wider narratives of decline. The implications for confidence and direction of a prolonged period out of power would persist and 'Labour's return to power did not convince everybody that all its problems had disappeared' (Fielding, 2003, p.36).

In opposition, the Conservative Party, which from 1965 was led by Edward Heath, was beginning to move away from the previous political consensus and to develop a set of ideas relating to free markets and small government. However, the party was unused to the opposition after 13 years in government and it included several high-profile figures, such as Enoch Powell, who tended to stray beyond their brief, pushing further from the prevailing opinions of the time and creating clear tensions within the party on issues such as incomes policy (Caines, 2017; Gamble, 1974). This would be a tumultuous period for the Conservative Party that continued from 1964, through later periods of government and then further opposition until the arrival in government of Margaret Thatcher and 'Thatcherism' in 1979. However, while these changes would come to have significant consequences, at this time there was not a clear direction for opposition (or for the party's up to 36 different policy groups) and the key political institutions in place at the time of the Bolton Committee's formation were those that had arisen from the period of political consensus.

Political Consensus and the NEDC

A significant outcome of the political consensus that had developed since the Second World War was the creation of the NEDC. It was, in 1962, a Conservative government rather than a socialist Labour administration that established the NEDC, building on similar organisations that had existed since the 1930s (Dell, 1997). Announced by Chancellor of the Exchequer Selwyn Lloyd in July 1961, the new body was formed through negotiation and held its first meeting in March 1962 (Meadows, 1978; Middlemas, 1983). The NEDC was a tripartite body comprising government and peak organisations representing both organised industrial and labour interests. The NEDC sought to coordinate economic activities and to address the country's economic decline through a set of ambitious targets for national growth. This work was further extended through the 'little neddies', the Economic Development Committees (EDCs) that focused on specific industries. Reinforcing the consensus for this coordinated approach to government and industry, the incoming Labour administration of 1964 largely continued Conservative plans (Meadows, 1978; Dell, 1997).

The Labour government set out its intentions for the NEDC with the National Plan (1965). This sought to utilise central planning to address what was perceived as the country's balance of payments problem and to set out an economic growth target centred on a 25% increase in national output between 1964 and 1970. As well as indicating the role for the NEDC, the Plan set out an important role for the 13 EDCs in existence at that time to facilitate the delivery of the Plan through the firms of each industry. These efforts were focused on improving the trade balance and increasing industrial efficiency.

The National Plan included discussion of what was referred to as 'industrial management', an area where 'Government are already providing support for a great deal of this work and will continue to take a close and active interest in it', including the promotion of greater 'professionalisation' (p.9). There was a shift in emphasis in economic policy towards a greater prominence for productivity as the answer to the country's problems. This included the Ministry of Labour becoming the

Department of Employment and Productivity. Productivity had indeed been lower than the majority of the UK's international competitors, and this trend would continue into the 1970s (Matthews, 2007).

In seeking to address the challenge of productivity, ideas of rationalisation continued to be influential in achieving increased efficiency. This was seen as requiring the promotion of mergers and a requirement for 'Various industries, including machine tools, electrical engineering and wool textiles, [to] examine their structure to see where rationalisation and larger units would increase competitive efficiency' (p.18). There were concerns that in industries with too many small firms would be significant inefficiencies. For example, Tomlinson (2004, p.109) cites documentation from the Ministry of Technology: 'Small firms cannot always support design and development teams adequate to modern needs and too many make inefficient use of skilled workers.' Nonetheless, beyond rationalisation, the overall focus was on working at the industry level rather than particular firms or with any focus on the size of firms. Indeed, part of a problem perceived with this planning approach and engagement with 'industry' concerned insufficient contact between government and individual firms (Tomlinson, 2004).

An important part of the government machinery for driving efficiencies was the Industrial Reorganisation Corporation (IRC), launched in 1966. The IRC was established to facilitate the reorganisation of industries or aid the development of an industrial enterprise, including through mergers (Pass, 1971). Despite efforts to stress the independence of the IRC from government, there remained concerns about increasing State intervention. More generally, there were concerns that the general framework of which the IRC formed a part, including the Monopolies Commission and NEDO, represented '[T]he 'powerlessness of the individual in the face of the bureaucrat ...' (Wills, 1969, p.40).

A further element of the plan to remedy the nation's relative economic decline, and achieve the growth targets, focused on improving the skills of Britain's workforce. The effort was to be arranged under industrial training boards but, Pemberton (2004) argues, the initiative largely foundered on the fragmented institutional landscape of government departments, industry bodies and labour representatives. While there seems to have been widespread acknowledgement of the problem, and agreement in the peak organisations that it needed to be addressed, there was difficulty in creating sufficient agreement to drive change and, among smaller firms, opposition because the introduction of 'a training levy would end their free-riding' (Pemberton, 2004, p.1000). Tomlinson (2004, p.129) suggests that the 'hostility' of small firms towards the industrial training boards played an important role in the establishment of the Bolton Committee.

The CBI and the Representation of Business

Among the peak organisations constituting the NEDC was the CBI. The CBI was formed in 1965 through the merger of three existing employers' organisations, in response to the perceived need for the effective representation of industry opinion (Grant and Marsh, 1977). This consolidation was supported by those who wanted a counterweight to the Trades Union Congress (TUC) and by a Labour government seeking effective means of discussion and planning with industry. In operating a regional structure, the CBI sought to perform 'the dual function of acting as a sounding board for industrial opinion on national and local matters, and facilitating personal contact between head office and the membership' (Grant and Marsh, 1971, p.405).

The CBI was generally focused on the large business concerns that were also the focus of government interventionist policy. Grant and Marsh (1977, p.37) record the 1973 membership revenue of the CBI where over 50% came from large industrial companies (>1,000 employees). Nonetheless, the National Association of British Manufacturers' (NABM) inclusion in the merger meant that the new organisation had a substantial small business membership and these business owners increasingly demanded more of a voice (the predominant smaller business membership also having made initial inclusion of NABM particularly challenging). Some small business owners felt that the ways in which the new arrangement centred on the CBI marginalised organisations such as the Association of British Chambers of Commerce (ABCC). This meant small business voices would not be heard and that their problems would not be given due emphasis (Bennett, 2011).

Lobbying the Government for Action on Small Business

In the post-war period, there had been an increasing role played by the State in economic and social matters and, through the development of institutions such as the NEDC, a process of concentration in resources in the private sector and trade unions. McHugh (1979, p.46) argued that this 'collectivist trend' represented

> an era increasingly dominated by 'big' business, interventionist government and powerful trade unionism, the small independent

entrepreneur, the typical representative of the petits-bourgeois has become a marginal social and economic category threatened by powerful political and economic forces.

Sentiment among small business owners regarding their relative prosperity and status had been noted as declining, since at least the early days of the Macmillan administration (Middlemas, 1986) and it is perhaps unsurprising that such a context would lead to the development of 'a small business sector consciousness' (Middlemas, 1990, p.182). These businesses often had significant doubts about the CBI and the effectiveness of its representation of their interests. This can be clearly seen in the formation of the Society of Independent Manufacturers, which went on to become the Smaller Businesses Association (SBA), adopting a more combative, 'drum beating' relationship with government than the CBI (Grant and Marsh, 1975, p.96).

The SBA expressed concerns about the diminished position of small businesses in the national economy and, in its first declaration of intent, challenged the established order of government-industry relations:

> Government interference in business is growing and to make matters worse, there is an increasing and alarming tendency for Big Government to speak to Big Business ... Behind this decision to speak only to Big Business is the idea that small companies are inefficient, incompetent and unable to export, and powerless politically.
>
> (BT360/4/1/ANNEX D, TNA, *The Times*)

The small business lobby became increasingly vocal under the leadership of the SBA and influential supporters such as Bernard Weatherill, Conservative MP. Weatherill was the co-author of the Conservative pamphlet *Acorns to Oaks*, which argued for the importance of sustaining a small business sector for economic flexibility (Weatherill and Cope, 1969). Weatherill and Cope set out their case for government policy to account for small businesses, contrasting the small business agencies of Japan, the United States and Germany with the absence of such agencies in Britain. The introduction to the pamphlet noted how interest in the small firm had been increasing, with the founding of the SBA and a small firms committee in the CBI, not to mention some signs of action from the government. They continued to argue, however, that simply removing the burdens of government legislation was insufficient. They appealed to the Conservative Party to 'go further and give positive help to small businesses as their colleagues abroad have done' (p.13).

Weatherill and Cope (1969) envisaged an organisation established as a government-funded body, with a Minister responsible to Parliament for overseeing its success and use of public funds, but as independent of government as possible. This new Bureau would 'exist to serve without fee or reward and it will be available to any firm qualified by size who wishes to use it' (p.14). They argued that, once established, the Bureau should seek to support the existence of a diverse population of small firms and provide policies and schemes for their benefit. This agenda could be fulfilled by the Bureau offering advice and support to small firms in areas such as finance, marketing and management. Within the machinery of government, the Bureau could operate a scheme to allocate a proportion of government contracts to small firms as well as giving voice to the difficulties of firms to enhance understanding among the government and the general public.

Brief mention of such an idea had featured in the Conservative 1966 election manifesto, which promised to 'Set up a Small Business Development Bureau to help small firms start and grow'. It would come to be an important part of the discussions of the Bolton Committee.

The CBI Calls for an Inquiry

With increased political attention on small businesses, the CBI faced pressure to demonstrate more clearly its commitment to representing the interests of its 5,000 small business members and many others connected via trade associations (McHugh, 1979). In 1966, the CBI set up a Steering Group for Small Firms that later evolved into a fully fledged council and, ultimately, into today's Enterprise Forum. The clearer positioning of a designated focal point for the concerns of 'small firms' as a constituency supported calls for action on their behalf.

In June 1968, CBI Director-General John Davies, addressing the British Federation of Master Printers, observed that 'the small businessman' might feel that their room for manoeuvre 'is being malevolently invaded' through burdens imposed by government. Davies pointed to 'an excess of industrial theorising in government rather than a pernicious and determined attack upon the small business' (CBI, 1968) and called for immediate action to relieve pressures on small firms pending further information to be gathered on their position in the economy. The CBI also published research to demonstrate the economic contribution of small firms and to characterise the government as misunderstanding them (CBI, 1968).

Anthony Crosland, now President of the Board of Trade for the Labour government, met with Davies, fully aware of the pressures on the CBI to demonstrate commitment to its small firm members (BT360/4/1,

TNA). Davies set out the CBI position on the areas of particular irritation for small businesses, including estate duty, shortfall assessments, company law and free depreciation (BT360/4/2, TNA). Reflecting a widely held attitude of the time towards small firms (Galbraith, 1972; Bannock, 1989), records indicate that Crosland was reluctant to intervene, especially in terms of indiscriminate support for all small firms (e.g. including less dynamic firms). Nevertheless, during the autumn of 1968, the CBI persisted in lobbying the Labour government through its role in the NEDC.

The CBI argued that legislation formed with large corporations in mind was creating significant burdens on small firms in respect of fiscal legislation and the requirements established under the Companies Act, industrial training rules and administrative requests from government (BT360/4/15, TNA). The CBI was calling for immediate concessions to small firms and for a study of how far small firms required separate legislative provisions, how existing legislation ought to be adjusted in content or application and what changes were required in government to better appreciate the needs of small firms. By December, records from the Treasury reflected the impression that Ministers were more or less committed to some form of activity in respect of small firms (T328/235, TNA).

With an apparent acceptance that an inquiry would be held in some form, civil servants started work on establishing its focus. According to a Board of Trade draft paper from December 1968, summarising events to date, the government favoured an inquiry oriented towards supporting dynamic and specialist firms as well as recognising the positive role of government policy: what government was already doing, how it could be more effective and what more could be done (BT360/5/1, TNA).

The CBI played an active role in the ongoing negotiations around the form of an inquiry, laying emphasis on the problems of small manufacturers and the question of corporation tax, which it was already discussing with the Inland Revenue. Records indicate that while it initially made use of its position as part of the NEDC, it is particularly interesting that the CBI also sought to exclude the tripartite function from serious influence. For example, the CBI rejected a proposal for a working party of the NEDC's offices to consider the problems of small firms on the grounds that it would require TUC involvement. For its part, the paper notes that the TUC did not favour the work being undertaken through the NEDC offices, reportedly on the grounds that the proposal 'was only C.B.I. propaganda and it would be a waste of NEDC's time to study the subject' (BT360/5/1, TNA).

Populating a Committee

By mid-February 1969, Crosland was outlining to John Diamond, Chief Secretary to the Treasury, the impasse reached in respect of the proposed inquiry. The CBI wanted an independent, committee-led inquiry, sponsored by the Board of Trade, headed by a prominent businessman to study the particular problems of small businesses (BT360/5/ 33, TNA). Meanwhile, the Treasury and the Inland Revenue preferred an academic-led, single person inquiry to gather the facts on small businesses' situation on the grounds that an academic would be less subject to political lobbying (BT360/5/11, TNA).

Crosland asked whether the Treasury might come around to the CBI position if the parties were able to agree on names of people for the inquiry and re-emphasised the government's desire for harmony with the CBI, noting:

> The matter has been under discussion for several months – the small business members of the CBI are clearly getting restive – and if we could all register our agreement on the form of the enquiry at the NEDC meeting in early March we would avoid any possibility of a row at that meeting which might damage unnecessarily our relations with the CBI.
>
> (BT360/5/39, TNA)

The Chief Secretary's reply of 31 March 1969 noted that, following the Chancellor's private discussions with Crosland and with Davies, the Treasury was content with a small committee of inquiry (BT360/6/ 1a, TNA).

To form the Committee, the CBI offered a list of acceptable chairmen, including eventual Chair John Bolton. As Andrew Thomson's (2016) biography of Bolton makes clear, his combination of achievements and experiences equipped him to be credible with both the business community and the Board of Trade. Bolton was credited with growing a successful small business, Solartron, and had fulfilled positions such as Chairman of the Council of the British Institute of Management, the Economic Development Committee for the Rubber Industry and Vice Chairman of the Royal Commission on Local Government in England.

The CBI listed other acceptable members such as Lawrence Tindale, General Manager of the Industrial and Commercial Finance Corporation (ICFC). The ICFC was founded in July 1945 as part of the continuing attempt to address the Macmillan Gap (see Chapter 2), representing the 'first significant attempt by the state to bridge the equity gap ...' (Lonsdale, 1997, p.38). Tindale would go on to become a Committee member. Reflecting wider consultation on the formation of the Committee, the British Institute of Management provided a shortlist of possible committee members including Edward Robbins, an engineer and consultant also suggested by Bolton, who would go on to join the Committee.

It was soon agreed by the CBI that Bolton would be approached to Chair the Committee and Professor Brian Tew, a highly respected economist from Nottingham University, was proposed by the government for the academic role, with both men accepting their invitations.

Agreeing the Terms of Reference

By mid-May 1969, the terms of reference had been agreed by the CBI and Treasury and, following informal consultation, the ABCC and TUC were reported to have raised no comments (BT360/6/33, TNA). Despite the progress that had been made in agreeing the terms and the structure and leadership of the Committee, pressure remained on the Board of Trade for early results. On 5 June, *The Daily Telegraph* reported the CBI's view 'that the investigation could be completed in about six months' and that 'much of the fact-finding work had already been done as a result of previous investigations'.

Bolton met with Crosland in mid-June 1969. The President's briefing notes prior to the meeting indicate the view that there was limited evidence concerning the particular effects of recent government policies on small firms. In addition, there was a desire expressed that an inquiry would not become simply a forum for complaints. Moreover, the notes express the wish that an inquiry would also recognise where government action had been positive and where government action to support small firms might be used more effectively and what new supports might be put in place. An illustrative list of topics was provided, including the importance of small firms in the economy, government provision to support small firms and the impact of government regulatory and administrative requirements (BT360/6/41a, TNA).

The notes of the meeting indicate that Bolton left the impression that he believed the facts on small businesses' problems were already well known via work conducted through the EDCs and other bodies and that the solution lay in a US-style Small Business Administration. Nevertheless, while potentially satisfying the CBI's reported eagerness for a quick report and follow-up actions, Bolton reportedly raised a concern over how much could be achieved in the 12-month time scale indicated by the Board of Trade, given the draft terms of reference.

A comprehensive and wide-ranging inquiry could occupy 10 years of work, while a 12-month timeframe would mean working from existing information (BT360/6/42, TNA). These issues would continue to be a central tension in the work of the Committee.

The convening of the Committee of Inquiry on Small Firms, with members Bolton, Tew, Tindale and Robbins, was announced via a written answer from Crosland to Labour backbench MP Eric Moonman on 23 July 1969 in which he outlined the finalised terms of reference:

> To consider the role of small firms in the national economy, the facilities available to them and the problems confronting them; and to make recommendations. For the purpose of the study a small firm might be defined broadly as one with not more than 200 employees, but this should not be regarded as a rigid definition.
>
> In the course of the study it will be necessary to examine in particular the profitability of small firms and the availability of finance. Regard should also be paid to the special functions of small firms, for example as innovators and specialist suppliers.
>
> (HC Deb (1969a) 787 c382W)

The Committee's creation was also noted verbally in the House of Commons by Board of Trade Minister of State Edmund Dell. Dell was defending the Labour government's record on recognising the problems of small firms against the charge that 'the massacre which is going on of small businesses is a policy of this Socialist Government in order to feed their sacred cow, nationalisation and more nationalisation' (HC Deb (1969b) col.1925, 23 July 1969).

Conclusion

The years of the 1960s leading up to the founding of the Committee of Inquiry on Small Firms resist any simple division between Right and Left politics. At the start of the decade, it was the Conservatives who created the NEDC, which was criticised as being a platform for advancing the interests of big business and interventionist governments, while the decade ended with a Labour government establishing an inquiry into the position of small firms.

Of course, a great deal changed during the decade, including the emergence of a louder voice for the interests of small firms. The creation of the SBA, CBI interest in the concerns of small businesses and political pledges towards these businesses all indicate how small firms were viewed as being of increasing importance politically, albeit from a low base. The creation of the Committee, and its particular focus, was the product of negotiation, including over who was to form the group. Ultimately, the Committee incorporated deep expertise and experience from a number of perspectives, each member contributing their own specialism.

Despite the views reported from some quarters, that the problems of small firms were already well understood and that a relatively short inquiry could suffice, it would quickly become apparent that this was far from the case. In Chapters 4 and 5 we go on to explore and discuss the sheer scale of the task confronting the Committee when it came to making sense of the small firms 'sector' and addressing the terms of reference provided for the Committee. Needless to say, the size of task loomed larger than seems to have been anticipated.

References

Bannock, G. (1989). Changing viewpoints. In: G. Bannock and A. Peacock (eds.) *Governments and small business*. London: Paul Chapman Publishing, pp.12–23.

BBC News (1957). Britons 'have never had it so good' On this Day 1950–2005, 20th July 1957. URL: http://news.bbc.co.uk/onthisday/hi/dates/stories/july/20/newsid_3728000/3728225.stm Accessed 01.05.21.

Bennett, R. (2011). *Local business voice: The history of Chambers of Commerce in Britain, Ireland, and revolutionary America 1760–2011*. Oxford: Oxford University Press.

BT360/4/1, TNA: Brief for the President for a discussion with Mr John Davies of the CBI on 9 July about the problems of small businesses and their role in the economy.

BT360/4/1/ANNEX D, TNA, *The Times*. George Clark, 'Small businessmen form political lobby' *The Times*, 10 May 1968.

BT360/4/2, TNA: Meeting with Mr John Davies about the problems of small companies, 11 July 1968.

BT360/4/15, TNA: NEDC Memorandum by the CBI 'The problem of the small firm'.

BT360/5/1, TNA: Draft Paper for INO(B) The Problem of the Small Firm, Note by The Board of Trade, December 1968.

BT360/5/11, TNA: Small Businesses, 10 December 1968.

BT360/5/33, TNA: The Small Business: Follow-up of the NEDC discussion on 7 October 1968.

BT360/5/39, TNA: Letter from Crosland to Diamond, 17 February 1969.

BT360/6/1a, TNA: Letter from Diamond to Crosland, 31 March 1969.

BT360/6/33, TNA: Enquiry into Small Businesses, 19 May 1969.

BT360/6/39, TNA: *The Daily Telegraph*, 'Speed small companies probe – CBI' 5 June 1969.

34   *From Little Acorns*

BT360/6/41a, TNA: Brief for the President's meeting with Mr John Bolton on 19 June 1969.

BT360/6/42, TNA: Note of a meeting: Enquiry into Small Firms, 20 June 1969.

Butler, D. (1995). *British General Elections since 1945* (2nd edition). Oxford: Blackwell, Oxford (Institute of Contemporary British History).

Caines, E. (2017). *Heath and Thatcher in opposition*. London: Palgrave.

CBI (1968). *Britain's small firms: Their vital role in the economy*. London: CBI.

Craig, F.W.S. (1990). *British General Election manifestos 1959–1987* (3rd edition). Aldershot: Parliamentary Research Services, Dartmouth (publisher).

Crosland, C.A.R. (1956). *The future of socialism*. London: Cape.

Dell, E. (1997). *The Chancellors: A history of the Chancellors of the Exchequer, 1945–90*. London: Harper-Collins.

Dunleavy, P. (1989). The United Kingdom: Paradoxes of an ungrounded statism. In: F. Castles (ed.) *The comparative history of public policy*. Cambridge: Polity, pp.242–291.

Fielding, S. (2003). *The Labour governments 1964–1970: Labour and cultural change*. Manchester: Manchester University Press.

Galbraith, J.K. (1972). *The new industrial state* (2nd edition). Harmondsworth: Penguin Books.

Gamble, A. (1974). *The Conservative nation*. London and New York: Routledge & Kegan Paul.

Grant, W.P. and Marsh, D. (1971). The Confederation of British Industry. *Political Studies*, 19(4): 403–415.

Grant, W.P. and Marsh, D. (1975). The politics of the CBI: 1974 and after. *Government and Opposition*, 10(1): 90–106.

HC Deb (1969a) vol.787 c382W. Anthony Crosland MP, written answer to Eric Moonman MP, 'Small Firms (Committee of Inquiry)', 23 July.

HC Deb (1969b) vol.787 col.1925. James Dance, MP, 23 July 1969.

Kavanagh, D. and Riches, C. (2016). *A dictionary of political biography* (2nd edition). Online version: Oxford University Press, eISBN: 9780191751080

LAB 8/3369, TNA: Extract from Women's Employment Survey, March 1968. URL: www.nationalarchives.gov.uk/wp-content/uploads/2014/03/lab8-33691.jpg Accessed 01.05.21.

Lonsdale, C. (1997). *The UK equity gap: The failure of government policy since 1945*. Aldershot: Ashgate Publishing.

Marsh, D. and Grant, W.P. (1977). *The Confederation of British Industry*. London: Hodder & Stoughton.

Matthews, D. (2007). The performance of British manufacturing in the post-war long boom. *Business History*, 49(6): 763–779.

McHugh, J. (1979). The self-employed and the small independent entrepreneur. In: R. King and N. Nugent (eds.) *Respectable rebels*. London: Hodder and Stoughton, pp.46–75.

Meadows, P. (1978). Planning. In: F.T. Blackaby (ed.) *British economic policy 1960–1974*. Cambridge: Cambridge University Press, pp.402–417.

Middlemas, K. (1983). *Industry, unions and government: Twenty-one years of NEDC*. London and Basingstoke: National Economic Development Council and Macmillan Press.

Middlemas, K. (1986). *Power, competition and the state (Vol. 1) Britain in search of balance, 1940–1961.* London: The Macmillan Press.

Middlemas, K. (1990). *Power, competition and the state, volume 2: Threats to the postwar settlement: Britain, 1961–74.* Houndmills: Macmillan.

Pass, C. (1971). The Industrial Reorganisation Corporation – a positive approach to the structure of industry. *Long Range Planning,* 4 (1): 63–70.

Pemberton, H. (2004). Relative decline and British economic policy in the 1960s. *The Historical Journal,* 47(4): 989–1013.

T328/235, TNA: Internal memo, 9 December 1968.

The National Plan (1965). Presented to Parliament by the First Secretary of State and Secretary of State for Economic Affairs, Cmnd. 2764, H.M.S.O.

Thomson, A. (2016). *Small business, education and management: The life and times of John Bolton.* Abingdon: Routledge.

Tomlinson, J. (2004). *The Labour Governments 1964–1970: Economic policy.* Manchester: Manchester University Press.

Tomlinson, J. (2016). De-industrialization not decline: A new meta-narrative for post-war British history. *Twentieth Century British History,* 27(1): 76–99.

Weatherill, B. and Cope, J. (1969). *Acorns to Oaks: A policy for small business.* London: Conservative Political Centre.

Who's Who (2007). *Who's who (Online), Who's who & Who was who.* Oxford: Oxford University Press.

Wills, G. (1969). "IRC... total success partial failure?" *Management Decision,* 3(2): pp.39–41.

4 Searching for Answers
Listening to Small Firms and Other Stakeholders

Introduction

In the period leading up to the Bolton Committee's formation, both the Confederation of British Industry (CBI) and incoming Committee Chair John Bolton appeared to consider the problems facing small firms to be well known. As we detailed in Chapter 3, the CBI therefore maintained pressure on the Board of Trade for early results. However, the confidence in the strength of existing understanding of the problems in the sector was brought into doubt as the Committee began to get to grips with its task. As acknowledged in the final report, 'It soon became obvious that we had undertaken a massive task, and one of great difficulty, for the small firm sector is extremely large and remarkably heterogeneous' (1971, p.xv).

While enterprise policy was small in scale in the UK, there were examples of international alternative approaches. Overseas visits were arranged to Japan, Canada, the United States, France and Germany to learn what other governments were doing on small business policy. Nevertheless, the majority of the Committee's early work was focused domestically on three main areas: existing statistical data, a large-scale survey and inviting submissions of evidence from small firms and other stakeholders. In this chapter, we discuss the collection and analysis of these data in each of these areas and highlight the challenges this work faced, especially in trying to meet an initially tight deadline for completion of the Committee's work.

The Committee Begins Its Work: Existing Statistical Data

From its first meeting on 23 July 1969, the Committee adopted a strong orientation towards action (BT262/20/CSF2, TNA). However, the terms of reference were broad (see Chapter 3) and members had to seek

DOI: 10.4324/9781003119142-4

a clear direction for their work. The minutes indicate that recourse was therefore had to the Board of Trade's suggested areas of focus. These were provided in a list of illustrative topics the Committee might consider that was included in the briefing notes for Crosland's meeting with Bolton to discuss his taking up the role of Committee Chair (BT360/6/41a, TNA). The list centres on the themes of: the role of small firms in the economy; the services provided to small firms by government and government-sponsored agencies along with levels of take up; and the particular implications for small firms of government requirements, such as those arising through the Industrial Training Act 1964 and form filling. Plans were also laid to take soundings from government departments and other institutions for their views on the general direction to be taken by the Committee.

It was agreed by the Committee that the inquiry would need to establish a statistical description of the small firm population. A statistics subcommittee was therefore established under Tew to gather and analyse data to identify trends and to test various propositions about small firms, such as their relatively high profitability compared to large firms. It was considered that gathering the general information on the small firm population could begin right away through 'examination of existing statistics on small firms, and those which can be readily obtained from Government Departments, universities and other institutions' (BT262/20/CSF2, TNA). The more complex testing of propositions was expected to require the commissioning of specialist research but, more fundamentally, that 'this could not usefully be started until the Committee had identified the problems they wished to investigate' (BT262/20/CSF2, TNA).

However, even the apparently simpler task of basic descriptive data proved to be difficult. The statistical evidence base held by government on small firms was extremely limited, reflecting the extent to which the focus on small firms as a category was a recent priority and out of step with the operation of government at the time. The National Plan (1965, p.18), for example, had focused on industries rather than size categories for its analysis of the economy and had indicated that 'Government will assist in the promotion of mergers ...' in efforts to rationalise industries and achieve competitive levels of efficiency through increased scale of units. Commenting on the period, Boswell (1973), previously of the Industrial and Commercial Finance Corporation, noted a lack of attention paid to small firms and understanding them.

The state of available data appears to have been an area of difficulty for the Committee (see, e.g. BT262/59, TNA; BT262/20/CSF9, TNA). Presenting an overall statistical view of small firms in the economy was hampered by the generally patchy data about the economy (BT262/26/21, TNA). The Inland Revenue could provide figures on numbers of small firms for 1967/8 based on using the size of profits as a proxy for the 'less than 200 employees' threshold defined by the Committee's terms of reference. However, providing figures for pre-1964/5 was not possible owing to the nature of the previous tax regime. Other statistics were pieced together from the Board of Trade 1963 Census of Production figures for Manufacturing and Construction, while detail on other industries could be taken from other years (BT262/20/CSF9, TNA; also BT262/25/39, TNA).

In seeking to understand the available data, and the idea that the collection of these data created a burden on small firms, the Committee engaged with stakeholders from within the civil service. On the matter of form filling and its associated burdens, evidence from the Central Statistical Office (CSO) appeared to emphasise the distinction between *statistical* forms and *administrative* forms. While the CSO was sympathetic to the general burden of form filling, the statistical form filling demands placed on the very smallest of firms was relatively light. The burdens created by other kinds of paperwork requesting information from small firms stemmed from other departments. Nevertheless, as pointed out by the Committee during a meeting with CSO representatives, from the perspective of small firm owners, the distinction between types of form mattered little (BT262/59, TNA).

By early December 1969, Tew was noted as reporting to the Committee that 'occasional meetings of the Statistics Sub-Committee had not proved the right instrument for collecting and collating the statistics' (BT262/20/CSF77, TNA). Early in the Committee's efforts, therefore, it was apparent that, contrary to claims that problems were already well known and represented a sufficient basis for action, there was as yet an incomplete picture of what a small firms 'sector' looked like.

Surveying Small Firms

In addition to exploring existing data, the Committee set to work designing a survey questionnaire to gather information (BT262/20/CSF9, TNA). Meanwhile, the CBI and Association of British Chambers of Commerce (ABCC) had moved quickly to prepare their own respective membership surveys for September 1969. In meeting the ABCC, the Committee expressed some concerns over the potential for duplication with the Committee's survey and negative effects on response rates (BT262/20/CSF26, TNA). The ABCC agreed that, when sending its own survey to the organisation's membership, it would include a note urging them to also complete the Committee's survey when that arrived.

The ABCC had found itself marginalised with the establishment of the National Economic Development Council (NEDC) and the formation of the CBI (Bennett, 2011). Now, although consulted during the formation of the Bolton Committee, the ABCC had expressed its disappointment (BT360/5/1, TNA) at being excluded from discussions on the Committee's establishment. For its part, the CBI continued to be criticised by the Smaller Businesses Association (SBA) for being out of touch with small firms: 'The Government speaks to the CBI, to Trade Organisations and to those in the NEDC, none of whom are aware of the full range of the problems of the smaller business' (SBA, n.d.).

Against the backdrop of these more or less explicit challenges to their relevance in respect of small firms, both the ABCC and the CBI sought to underline their influence in founding the Bolton Committee (T326/1225, TNA). In its letter to members accompanying a survey in September 1969, the ABCC explained the efforts of local Chambers over the years to fight the cause for small firms and it was with the approval of the ABCC that the Bolton Committee had been established. For its part, the CBI accompanied its own small business questionnaire with a letter explaining that it was the CBI that had moved to have the government establish the Bolton Committee. Furthermore, it was noted that the Committee was adopting the CBI definition of 'small firm'.

Consistent with its initial 12-month time scale, over the summer of 1969 the Committee produced a survey for small businesses, despite Bolton reportedly feeling that 'the Committee's research aims were yet to be defined with precision' (BT262/20/CSF53, TNA). Further, the survey was developed at haste by the Committee with support from the Department of Trade and Industry and the Business Statistics Office, foregoing 'the pilot of testing stages, which are otherwise usual in a survey of this type' (Research Unit, 1972, p.1).

The government's Business Statistics Office selected the sample of 15,800 small businesses for the survey and managed its distribution, response handling and initial analyses (Research Unit, 1972, p.1). Before sampling, 'the population was stratified into 14 industrial groups, of which eight were in manufacturing and six in non-manufacturing. In addition, three size-groups (according to employment) were distinguished in manufacturing; in total, therefore, there were 30 strata' (ibid.). The survey that was received by firms contained two parts, Part One sought general information about the firm and Part Two requested detail on the firm's finances. Responses were due by 31 December 1969 and for Part

One, 3,500 usable responses were received, while for Part Two, 2,115 usable responses were received. Looking at this in greater detail:

> The response rate was higher in manufacturing than in non-manu-facturing (26 as against 19 per cent). Medium-sized firms, with 25–99 employees, showed a higher response rate than both smaller and larger firms (33 per cent compared with an average of 21 per cent).
>
> (ibid.)

Although achieving an impressive scale of data collection, acknowledged limitations around response bias, a non-representative sample and broadly framed questions served to limit the quality of data obtained. To give a sense of the potential problems in the Committee's survey data, the Research Unit cautioned that 'the questionnaire was relatively complex and a degree of ambiguity in response is inevitable' (ibid., p. 2). The cautions offered around the survey data were grounded in ana-lyses of the financial information provided, based on representative subsamples of 50 companies and 45 non-incorporated enterprises.

From the check undertaken, the Research Unit discovered that a small number of companies (4 out of 50) should have been excluded from the survey because they exceeded the size limits for the Committee's work or because they were subsidiaries of larger concerns. Further problems of how firms were classified were also detected along with how certain financial information had been presented, for instance profits before tax. Of particular interest, in light of comments about the clarity of questions posed, were the discrepancies between respondents' answers and their audited accounts. When it was possible to compare the accounts summarised by respondents to the questionnaire with what had been filed at Companies House (31 firms), 'significant discrepan-cies' were found in half of the cases (ibid., p. 2). In explaining the errors, the Research Unit attributed the problem, at least in part, to unclear instructions in the questionnaire over what items should be included.

Nevertheless, despite these acknowledged limitations and criticisms of the data gathered through the survey, the Committee members considered the tables drawn from the postal survey to be 'the best stat-istical analysis of the small firm sector ever attempted, and based on the largest sample ever used' (BT262/21/CSF372, TNA). Although the limitations meant that certain fine-grained analyses might not be developed from the data, they still offered the prospect of providing an overview of the sector and drawing some comparisons with large, quoted companies (Tamari, 1972). It was also noted that statistical data on large firms were not comprehensive at this point (BT262/21/

CSF347, TNA), indicating that some of the data challenges faced by the Committee were not necessarily specific to the study of small firms.

Survey Results

Results from the questionnaires were presented in two reports, *A Postal Questionnaire of Small Firms: Financial Data* (Tamari, 1972) and *A Postal Questionnaire of Small Firms: Non-Financial Data* (Research Unit, 1972) (The other research reports produced for the Committee are discussed in detail in Chapter 5). Tamari, an expert on small firms' accounts from the Bank of Israel's Research Department who supported the Committee's analyses during four months working at the Department of Trade and Industry, considered firms' accounting information based on the period 1964–1968.

The report draws out several interesting features regarding the financial position and structure of small firms. Respondents reported using 'more trade credit and less bank loans and overdrafts in relation to their sales and to their short-term financing' (Tamari, 1972, p.1), with trade credit being more expensive than bank credit. Tamari explains the roots of this higher cost structure in part owing to a preference among financial institutions for lending to large firms, which offer greater security and for which the loans are relatively cheaper to arrange. However, he also points to small firms' reluctance to take on the risk of substantial loan capital and notes that 'Of even greater interest is the fact that of all the firms surveyed only one-third had attempted to raise additional external finance' (ibid., p.2).

Although set against a backdrop of declining profitability in the period 1964–1968, for quoted firms as well as the small firms surveyed, Tamari reported that on average the small firms responding to the survey had higher profit ratios than quoted firms. Such a finding must be read against the acknowledged volatility facing small firms:

> Profitability is much more variable amongst small manufacturing firms than amongst large firms. This is consistent with what is known from other studies of the higher mortality rate among smaller firms; the greater risk of failure of some firms is compensated by the higher profitability rate of others.
>
> (ibid., p.4)

The report also provided insights into business growth. The fast-growing firms (manufacturing: sales growth of 15% a year; non-manufacturing: sales growth of 10% a year) comprised 11% of the study sample. Among the fast-growers, as compared to slow-growers, chief executives were more likely to be under 60 years of age and tended to rely more on borrowed funds. They also provided more credit to customers, which was thought to be a means of increasing sales, and they tended to be more profitable.

The Research Unit's report considered the non-financial data from the postal questionnaire. Its general overview of findings, drawn from their detailed tables of analysis, reported on 12 categories to offer a sense of small firms at that time. In terms of *legal status*, whereas small manufacturing firms were overwhelmingly private limited companies, among non-manufacturers around half of the firms were run by a sole proprietor. Considering the *number of owners* in responding firms, it was most common for there to be two partners who worked in the business and shared control. The *chief executive* was reported to often be 'the founder of the firm or a member of the founder's family' (1972, p. 3). From the information provided, we might also presume them to be mostly men.

In light of concerns discussed by the Committee about concentration in the economy and the role of small firms, it is interesting to note that for *sales and competition* small firms still tended to face competition from other small firms. Moreover, the survey analysis reported that a firm's largest customer would represent less than 25% of its total sales. While the government saw rationalisation as vital for efficiency and productivity gains, *mergers* activity appeared low, with up to 5% of respondents reporting a take-over of, or merger with, other firms during recent years. However, more broadly in relation to government modernisation agendas, a significant share of respondents among manufacturing firms reported making a major *innovation* in recent years, with product innovations and process innovations being identified.

In terms of people management practices in small firms, *training schemes*, in the form of on-the-job staff training, were provided by most firms, with this generally focused on operators rather than all staff. *Unionisation* rates among respondent firms were low as were memberships of employers' federations, with such memberships being more common among slower growing firms. The *selective employment tax* was reported as having led many non-manufacturing firms to reduce staff headcounts.

On business *finance*, between one half and two-thirds of all respondents reported using overdrafts, although many respondents reported having their overdraft limits reduced in the past year. Small firms reported providing *credit* to customers and also facing *liquidity* pressures, most commonly because of delayed payments from large customers. A third of the responding companies reported changing their *dividend distribution* policy in the light of the 1965 Finance Act, with most of these indicating that they had received professional advice on the changes required for compliance. As we discuss in Chapter 6, the understanding of provisions contained in the Finance Act and the quality of professional advice available to small firms were felt to have important shortcomings.

The overall value of the survey conducted by the Committee is simultaneously significant and questionable. Set within the context of limited knowledge on small firms at the time it was conducted, the questionnaire stands out as a significant achievement and it provides some useful information about small firms. The limitations contained within the work should also be understood within their proper context, with the Committee working to an initially short timeline creating pressure to release the survey. Nevertheless, understanding the reasons for the limitations does not remove them and so analyses based on the survey are necessarily to be treated with a degree of caution. Perhaps one of the most significant findings to arise from the survey concerns the heterogeneity of what they were studying as the small firms 'sector' and therefore revealing, or at least underlining, the complexity of the task the Committee had been charged with undertaking.

Submissions of Evidence

The Committee not only sought quantitative data but also to engage more qualitatively with the views and experiences of small firms and other stakeholders. Keenly aware of the timeframe for the work, an initial schedule was established that required submissions of evidence by the end of October 1969, with report drafting planned for February to April 1970. However, by the Committee's second meeting, trade associations had indicated that a late October deadline would be too tight and the Committee was still holding oral evidence gathering sessions in Autumn 1970 (BT262/20/CSF9, TNA).

Submissions of evidence were received from a broad range of stakeholders. The final Committee Report lists its evidence base as comprising representations from 91 trade associations, 25 general trade organisations, 58 professional, advisory and consultative organisations, 20 universities and technical colleges, 34 financial organisations, 21 government departments, 22 industrial training organisations in addition to a number of individual businesses and a range of other political and industry sources at home and internationally.

Submissions from Small Firms

The Committee received representations about small firms, as well as from those organisations positioning themselves as speaking on behalf of small firms. Some business owners contributed their views directly to the Committee and this correspondence reflects the heterogeneity of small firms as a sector such that it is hard to discern a representative view among small firms (BT262/69, TNA and BT262/70, TNA).

One correspondent explained that relatively complicated planning rules were hard to understand and, with little help from the local authorities, were unjust and forcing them out of business. Another correspondent, addressing Mr Bolton directly, reflected the apparent irony of a government department sending out a burdensome, and not especially appropriate, battery of questions to discover what burdens small firms felt placed under by government! (BT262/67, TNA).

Meanwhile, the records of Tew's visit to the North of England in mid-December 1969 identified other problems raised by the people he spoke to. The Industrial Training Act was generally described as creating unnecessary administrative burdens and the 'pantomime' of compliance (BT360/9/5/CSF84, TNA), while planning regulations created hassles rather than fundamental problems. In general, the submissions contributed on behalf of small firms drew on a common narrative of small firms as victims of challenging circumstances, often laying the blame for this on government or large businesses.

In one submission, for example, a national trade association stressed the harmful effects of government burdens on the environment for small businesses, with legislation and fiscal policy identified as damaging small firms (BT262/33/25a, TNA). Owing to the ways that such burdens fall on one person, or a few people, in a small firm, submissions argued that increased administrative requirements hamper businesses, especially by demanding management attention rather than energies being focused on running the business. As one business-owner submitted to the Committee, bureaucracy and interference from government was holding back small firms from improving efficiency and limiting the time they had to plan ahead for the business.

Others offered specific examples of how the current government requirements were burdensome and compared unfavourably with previous approaches to regulation, questioning the motivation behind such increases. Such burdens were also evidenced in some businesses' ability to participate in the Committee's work by submitting evidence. Having thanked the Committee for its letter inviting submissions some months prior, one correspondent was apologetic in explaining that their delay in responding simply reflected the pressures of routine tasks that fell on one or two people in a small business (BT262/67, TNA).

The London Chamber of Commerce, reporting on its own survey issued to inform its evidence to the Committee, recorded that its small business members were hampered in the prevailing credit squeeze. This evidence cited complaints such as how 'our debtors which are usually large concerns take much longer to pay, whereas our creditors are becoming more and more ruthless when enforcing their credit terms' and how 'One of the most pressing problems is the assumption by very large companies that small service companies can and should be able to provide several months (sic) credit' (BT262/37, TNA), a problem echoed among other contributors (BT262/69, TNA).

Submissions from other Stakeholders

Submissions from representative groups or other stakeholders reflected broader interests. In its oral evidence to the Committee, the SBA was keen to argue the case for its own existence on the basis of understanding small firms and having their interests at heart. Their representatives commented that:

> From reading other evidence we have seen which has been put to you, we get the impression that most of the people thought about the problem *ab initio* and then wrote round to their members. We were set up because most of the people who belong to us knew what it was about.
>
> [They continued:] ... with due respect to the CBI, I cannot see how you can represent big business, nationalised industries and small firms. The Companies Act is a case in point. You are bound to have a head-on collision.
>
> (BT262/38, TNA)

The fragmented nature of small business representation was of concern to the Committee and Bolton offered to support efforts that would deliver a more coordinated voice for these firms; still, in their final report the Committee chided small business representatives for failing to offer a united front (1971, p.93).

Discussing the need for advice and support among business owners, the ABCC offered the view that successful businesses would be able to find their way to free guidance as they needed it. Unsuccessful businesses would simply go out of business. There was no need to find ways of driving people to seek guidance. Elsewhere in the same discussion with the ABCC, a representative opined that 'small firms can have an in-built resistance to training'. Many small firms, he explained, '... think they do not need advice, they do not need training, they have got it all'. In view of this, when training brings with it associated financial and administrative burdens for the small firm, it creates resentment among small firms (BT262/38a, TNA).

Other stakeholders took the opportunity to promote the role they could play in future relationships between government and small businesses, indicating how the future of this policy agenda was viewed (BT360/9/79, TNA). For example, a regional productivity association was keen to emphasise its engagement with small firms and how local productivity associations were well-served to address the problems facing these firms (BT262/20/CSF79, TNA). Working in the context of an ongoing business advisory services review, the British Productivity Council (BPC) submission argued that it was already well-placed to address the problems facing small firms but that it would require more resources to extend its provision (the BPC was 75% funded by government 'grant-in-aid' and jointly sponsored by the CBI and TUC) (EW19/452, TNA).

Large business submissions recognised small firms as part of the mainstream economy, rather than inherently special. Small firms were often highlighted in these submissions as valuable parts of supply chains, for example where bespoke products or services were required. Nevertheless, idiosyncratic management and resource limitations were said to cause small firms difficulties in the face of complex projects or increased demand. While small firms represented a large proportion of customers, they were presented as contributing little to overall revenues.

The Consumer Council argued that: 'If small firms concentrate on their strong points then they have nothing to fear from the multiples and should not require special measures to help them to survive' (1970, p.1). Concerns were raised, for example, about special provisions that sought to protect small businesses through restricting the discounts manufacturers could grant to large-scale distributors, weakening disclosure requirements for small businesses that might benefit 'persistent defaulters' at the expense of consumers, and increasing the flexibility for trading agreements.

Doubts concerning the overall standard of business management in small firms were also expressed in relation to their ability to access finance. Evidence from finance organisations commented that money was available to sound businesses:

> if the management looks reasonably intelligent and if it is able to produce up-to-date figures then they would be able to get their credit in what is the cheapest way from their point of view either from their joint stock bank or on hire purchase or leasing.
>
> (BT262/54, TNA)

While some witnesses from within the finance sector downplayed the height of hurdles required of applicants, others gave accounts of the technical person who lacked commercial acumen (BT262/54/58, TNA). This trope of technically gifted founders without a head for modern management techniques or running a modern business (BT262/39/2, TNA) seems to have been well established in some quarters.

Committee member Robbins contributed, with some scepticism, that the Committee had received representations that small business owners were somehow 'going on cruises and spending vast sums of money gambling at Monte Carlo and all the rest of it' rather than 'ploughing that money back in for new machinery for future years' before questioning the grounds for efforts to 'convert them on some religious basis to want to improve their plant and machinery' (BT262/38a, TNA). Bolton himself, however, reflected that both the highly successful businesses and those doomed to fail were at the fringes. Of concern to the national interest were those businesses that could be more efficient. The businesses, for instance, being operated by someone working long hours who is too busy to get help:

> He may have come up as a craftsman, he may be a first class craftsman, but is scared to reveal his weaknesses certainly in the local circumstances so he is just a bit scared about going and admitting he does not know the run of the business which is what it is. It is these people who need a push to find out that they can be helped and that this is useful to the economy about whom we need to think.
>
> (BT262/38a, TNA)

Conclusion

From its early meetings, the Committee was faced with the consequences of a situation it was seeking to resolve; that small firms had not been a particular focus of governments. Working from such a starting point, the Committee had to be proactive in discovering more about the role of small firms and their experiences in the economy. Undertaking such a substantial exercise at speed meant that certain compromises were necessary, with implications for the overall quality of data obtained through the survey activity. Nevertheless, the scale of the activity undertaken cannot be overlooked nor can the helpful insights that were gathered on the basic demographics of small firms.

The other sources of information gathered by the Committee, through written and oral submissions, offer rich insights into the prevailing views of the day and how the Committee engaged with witnesses. Yet the volume of information received by the Committee also brought with it challenges of how it should be understood; for instance, in the absence of robust data, how could competing accounts be weighed against each other? This played out in terms of competing narratives that suggested a position of small firms as victims lacking a level playing field versus a counter-narrative of small firms as needing to look to improve their own management and they were not inherently special or unfairly disadvantaged.

Given the nature and scale of the challenge that lay ahead, it is unsurprising that the Committee moved to appoint a Research Director who would propose a programme of research to support the Committee's work. We turn to this further strand of work, published across multiple research reports, in Chapter 5.

References

Bennett, R. (2011). *Local business voice: The history of Chambers of Commerce in Britain, Ireland, and revolutionary America 1760–2011*. Oxford: Oxford University Press.

Bolton, J.E. (1971). *Committee of inquiry on small firms,* Cmnd. 4811. London: H.M.S.O. (reprint).

Boswell, J. (1973). *The rise and decline of small firms*. London: George Allen & Unwin.

BT262/20/CSF2, TNA: 1st Committee meeting, 23 July 1969.

BT262/20/CSF9, TNA: 2nd Committee meeting, 1 August 1969.

BT262/20/CSF26, TNA: 6th Committee meeting, 3 September 1969.

BT262/20/CSF53, TNA: 11th Committee meeting, 16 October 1969.

BT262/20/CSF77, TNA: 16th Committee meeting, 4 December 1969.

BT262/20/CSF79, TNA: 17th Committee meeting, 11 December 1969.

BT262/21/CSF347, TNA: 71st Committee meeting, 24 March 1971.

BT262/21/CSF372, TNA: 84th Committee meeting, 2 June 1971.

BT262/25/39, TNA: Committee of Inquiry on Small Firms: Note on a meeting on 20 November 1969 to discuss the availability of government statistics.

BT262/26/21, TNA: (file) Committee of Inquiry into Small Firms: Statistics.

BT262/33/25a, TNA: Trade association submission.
BT262/37, TNA: Evidence from London Chamber of Commerce, published February 1970.
BT262/38, TNA: 11th Evidence Hearing, 23 July 1970.
BT262/38a, TNA: 10th Evidence Hearing, 23 July 1970.
BT262/39/2, TNA: Business support organisation submission.
BT262/54, TNA: 45th Evidence Hearing, 21 September 1970.
BT262/54/58, TNA: Evidence Hearing (not numbered), 22 October 1970.
BT262/59, TNA: 47th Evidence Hearing, 21 September 1970.
BT262/67, TNA: Individual firms (submissions).
BT262/69, TNA: Individual firms (submissions).
BT262/70, TNA: Individuals (submissions).
BT360/5/1, TNA: Draft Paper for INO(B) the Problem of the Small Firm, Note by the Board of Trade, December 1968.
BT360/6/41a, TNA: Brief for the President's meeting with Mr John Bolton on 19 June 1969.
BT360/9/5/CSF84, TNA: Memo by Professor Tew on visit to West Riding, 15 and 16 December 1969.
BT360/9/79, TNA: Advisory Services and Consultancy Grants.
EW19/452, TNA: Evidence to the Committee of Inquiry on Small Firms, by the British Productivity Council, December 1969.
Research Unit (1972). *A postal questionnaire survey of small firms: Non-financial data, tables, definitions and notes.* London: H.M.S.O.
SBA (n.d.). *Britain's smaller businesses threatened.* London: Smaller Business (sic) Association (British Library).
T326/1225, TNA: Correspondence to their respective members from ABCC (3 September 1969) and the CBI (8 September 1969).
Tamari, M. (1972). *A postal questionnaire survey of small firms: An analysis of financial data.* London: H.M.S.O.
The Consumer Council (1970). The Consumer Council's submission to the Committee of Enquiry on Small Firms (Press Notice), 10 February (also BT262/40/14, TNA).
The National Plan (1965). Presented to Parliament by the First Secretary of State and Secretary of State for Economic Affairs, Cmnd. 2764. London: H.M.S.O.

5 Searching for Answers
The Committee's Data Collection Effort

Introduction

As the 'first comprehensive study, official or otherwise, of the small firm sector in the United Kingdom' (1971, p.xv), the Bolton Committee engaged in a major data-gathering exercise. The data-gathering effort grew in size and complexity as the challenging nature of the task facing the Committee became apparent. In addition to the analysis of existing statistical data, the large-scale survey and the submissions of evidence, the Committee commissioned 18 research reports. Although these reports, covering a wide range of concerns relevant to small firms, informed the Committee's deliberations and were published separately from the Committee's official report; they have received little if any focused attention.

Despite the challenges and acknowledged limitations, and further hindered by the time and resource constraints the research teams faced, the reports offer detailed snapshots of the small firms' landscape from the time. They underline not only the hurdles facing the research teams but also those encountered by the Committee members in their efforts to 'consider the role of small firms in the national economy, the facilities available to them and the problems confronting them; and to make recommendations' (1971, p.v). The reports also represent a major research effort with valuable findings for understanding small firms, with many points still resonating today.

In Chapter 4, our discussion of the Committee's survey focused on analyses presented in research reports 16 (Tamari, 1972) and 17 (Research Unit, 1972). Our focus in this chapter is expanded to consider the remaining 16 published research reports. We do this by firstly establishing the context in which the reports were created. We discuss in detail four important themes from the research reports' findings:

DOI: 10.4324/9781003119142-5

defining small firms; management of small firms; attitudes of owner-managers; and access to finance.

Appointing a Research Director

After the initial difficulties of working with the available statistical base together with the revealed complexity and heterogeneity of the small firms 'sector', the Committee's completion within the original timeframe was beginning to look unfeasible. Tew observed during a discussion on the outline of the Committee's report in December 1969 that 'Committee members had not thrashed out their views sufficiently on the subjects to be considered' (BT262/20/CSF/77, TNA). It was apparent that, contrary to initial expectations, existing knowledge of small firms was much more fragmented and uncertain than anyone had thought, indicating how overlooked these firms had been in policymaking.

The amount of work required to fulfil the Committee's remit and the constraints of the initial timeframe prompted discussions of what kind of report they were to produce. Minutes from the 16th Committee Meeting in early December 1969 (BT262/20/CSF77, TNA) indicate that members were agreed on the central task of the report, to identify the problems facing small firms and address them with recommendations. However, the minutes also reflect differing views on how detailed the description of the small firm sector ought to be. The minutes record that Robbins preferred to retain the current schedule of reporting in the following Autumn, even if that meant not every topic could be addressed. However, Tew and Tindale considered that a comprehensive report would be of the greatest value. Tew was reported to advocate a scholarly reference work on the topic, which could require adding one year to the Committee's duration. Given that this could not be achieved on the Committee's schedule, this would be something for the government to undertake following the report. For his part, Tindale is recorded as having expressed the view that a thorough piece of work would stand a greater chance of being taken seriously and being acted upon.

As the Chair, John Bolton, was absent from this meeting, resolving the discussion was postponed until the following meeting. At this time, it was clear that the report would not be expected ahead of a General Election, anticipated for Autumn of 1970 (we discuss this election and its implications for the Committee in detail in Chapter 6). As a result, the Committee's deadline for completing its work was revised to December 1970 with a view to publishing the report shortly thereafter (BT262/20/CSF79, TNA).

In line with this revised timetable, Tew emphasised the need for the appointment of a Research Director as soon as possible. The appointment of a Research Director represented a significant development for the Committee and its activities, moving away from the Committee's previously somewhat ad hoc approach. Although having sought a Research Director for some months, it was in late November that the Committee interviewed and agreed to offer the appointment to Graham Bannock, an economist and market researcher with experience at the OECD and in the automotive sector (BT262/20/CSF/71, TNA).

In its preliminary research report in February 1970, the Research Unit reaffirmed Tew's previous assessment of the limitations of existing data, noting the challenges posed such that, when pulled together, 'the resulting mosaic will be illuminating, [but] the lack of an adequate framework will remain a major deficiency.' (BT360/9/61a, TNA). Moreover, the diversity of small firms in respect of sector and motivations, among other factors, provoked important questions for consideration (ibid.).

Although time pressures remained a major concern, the Research Unit proposed a coordinated programme of research including a Treasury economist on secondment. Projects were prioritised where they were perceived to fill knowledge gaps on the economic role of small firms and to help the Committee decide whether, and how, small firms should be helped. On this basis, the research programme was approved in principle by the Committee in February 1970 (BT262/20/CSF106, TNA).

Placing the Research Reports in Context

The research reports were produced by civil servants, university researchers and private research firms. Several of them, in introducing their findings, drew attention to the difficulties experienced in conducting the research. Although these difficulties manifested in different ways, they reflect the relative lack of information gathered on small firms in the period leading up to the Committee's work.

Of course, small firms had not been entirely absent from research or government thinking in the preceding years. The 'Macmillan Gap' (discussed in Chapter 2 and dating from 1931) reflected some consideration of financing problems facing small firms, as did Lord Radcliffe's 1959 *Committee on the Working of the Monetary System*, although small firms were by no means central concerns in either of these committees. In the United States, Kaplan (1948, p.1) had set out to consider 'What is the role of small business in the economy? [and] How can small business be helped to contribute its full share to postwar employment and prosperity?' Hollander (1967, p.xvii) had been commissioned by the US Small Business Administration to study 'the impact of economic forces on small business'. Kaplan's and Hollander's works were cited in one of the Bolton Committee's research reports, Davis and Kelly's (1972) report on *Small Firms in the Manufacturing Sector*. There had also been work in the UK from researchers such as Woodward (1965/1980) who incorporated some small firms into her study of *Industrial Organization*. Important research was being published around the same time as the Bolton Committee's investigations, for instance, Ingham's study of *Size of Industrial Organization & Worker Behaviour* (1970, conducted 1964–1967) and Boswell's research (1969–1971) which was presented in *The Rise and Decline of Small Firms* (1973).

Boswell's research ran alongside that of the Committee, which was convened six months after Boswell's own project had started. As someone who had worked previously for the ICFC, Boswell worked from an informed perspective that can help explain the difficulties reported by some of those conducting research for the Bolton Committee. Boswell commented on 'a legacy of past disinterest' and how 'neither governments, academics or public commentators thought it worthwhile to go to much trouble in collecting the facts' (1973, p.14). Freeman (1971), notes in the very first paragraph of his report for the Committee on *The Role of Small Firms in Innovation in the UK since 1945* that 'the post-war debate on size of firm in relation to innovation, invention and research ... has been inconclusive because of the lack of adequate empirical evidence on the relative contribution of small firms to innovation.'

Lund and Miner (1971, p.51) presenting their analysis of *Three Studies on Small Firms* explained that:

> Very little statistical information currently exists on the performance of small firms in the United Kingdom economy. Official statistics tend to classify aggregate firm data by industry or region rather than by firm type or size. Indeed, although the National Income and Expenditure Blue Book classifies profits and capital formation by type of firm (personal and company sectors), no official statistical series is published classified by firm size.

A similar position was highlighted by Todd (1971, p.3) when setting out the landscape on *The Relative Efficiency of Small and Large Firms*: 'The volume of existing literature which deals with the subject on hand is extremely small. Empirical research into the efficiency of business units, and of small firms in particular, is almost non-existent.'

Defining the Small Firm

Related to the challenge of limited prior research, challenges persisted in defining what constituted a small firm for the purposes of the research projects. At one level, there were challenges concerning the relevance of the definition applied to the industry being studied. Lees and colleagues at the Economists Advisory Group (EAG) considered that the size of firm as defined by the Committee lacked relevance for the financial institutions being consulted so, with the Committee's agreement, they adopted 'rough equivalents of its definitions in terms of net assets and turnover' (1971, p.4).

In a study of *The Small Firm in the Motor Vehicle Distribution and Repair Industry*, Hebden and Robinson noted in 'Appendix A Size Classification' that they had 'not been able to retain the same classification system throughout the study and at times have referred to size in a rather loose manner' (1971, p.42). In this explanatory note, Hebden and Robinson go on to discuss the Committee's terms of reference which suggested that firms with an annual turnover of less than £100,000 should be categorised as small firms. They identify several problems with this categorisation for the motor trade, including the range of businesses:

> For instance, the turnover value of a car sales transaction is much larger than the average workshop transaction and consequently the turnover measure will indicate differences in size between the two activities that would not be so pronounced if size of plant or labour force measures were used.

Although the report authors could account for such intra-sector distinctions when collecting their own data, when drawing on prior research this was not always possible.

The challenge of intra-industry heterogeneity was also highlighted explicitly by Pickering et al. who investigated *The Small Firm in the Hotel and Catering Industry*. They explained that 'The "hotel and catering" industry is really a number of heterogeneous industries which happen to receive similar treatment in certain important respects from the government' (1971, p.3). There were important differences in terms of the economic conditions faced by different firms and the nature of the activities they conducted. Although the authors note that changes breaking down the industry into further categories had been incorporated into the 1968 revision of the Standard Industrial Classification, the range remained 'too broad for it to be suggested that one set of conclusions can apply with equal validity to all types of enterprise covered in each Minimum List Heading' (ibid.).

The problems of complexity and heterogeneity within the small firm 'sector' encountered in the initial work of the Committee, therefore, continued to provide significant challenges, even for research projects focused on specific industries.

Management in Small Firms

There is a general acknowledgement throughout the research reports that the conditions facing small firms around this time were tough. Taxation and government actions appeared to make matters worse rather than better. However, a theme repeated across a number of the reports addressed the perceived poor standard of management in small firms, echoing some of the oral testimony and general attitudes expressed to the Committee.

Davies and Kelly (1972) reported that the relatively high rate of failure for small firms could not be explained by the market or institutional discrimination against them. Rather, the decision of small business owners to enter intensely competitive sectors, with low barriers to entry, had an important role to play. The authors go on to identify that 'A second factor contributing to high failure rate is the ineptness of management' (p.62). Nevertheless, while emphasising the importance of potential business owners undertaking careful appraisals of their markets and their own managerial capabilities before launching a venture, Davies and Kelly note that 'it would be regrettable if such a rational appraisal reduced the supply of effective entrepreneurs' (ibid.).

The theme of management competence was further highlighted by concerns over business owners who found it relatively easy to enter trades, but then encountered stiff challenges. Smith (1971), writing one of two reports on retail commissioned by the Committee (also see Hall, 1971), highlights the general lack of formal training among those working in small retail establishments. Such a shortfall in formal training could leave the businesses ill-equipped to cope with changes in the sector. Interestingly, a similar account was provided of the hotel trade, in which small hotels and restaurants could be purchased without great difficulty by owners who lacked training and business orientation. A concern was highlighted that this could prove challenging where 'an increasingly sophisticated managerial and technological basis develops in the industry' (Pickering et al., 1971, p.80). Meanwhile, Hillebrandt (1971, p.52) considered that, in the construction industry, 'the scarcest resource and therefore greatest limit on the expansion of capacity is management' and that this was particularly the case amongst small firms.

The Attitudes of Owner-Managers

In relation to these views on the standard of management competence in various kinds of small firms, Golby and Johns' (1971) report on the *Attitude and Motivation* in small firms provided insight into how business owners themselves saw their challenges. This report set out to offer an in-depth study of the attitudes and motivation of small firm owners by exploring their views on a range of matters including areas of difficulty and the role of small firms in the economy more generally. The study, incorporating the views of 60 owners and nine managing directors with major shareholdings, was conducted via 14 non-directive group discussions held across England and Wales in Spring 1970.

Participants in the study identified finance and labour problems as those looming largest for small firms. Challenges presented by the 'credit squeeze' were explained as being exacerbated by large firms not paying their bills to small firms on time. Meanwhile, the labour problems were 'thought to be caused not only by the tax system which was seen as a disincentive to the extra effort of employees, but also by the 'Welfare State' which often paid better than the employer was able to' (ibid., p.4). Within this mix, government was perceived to be working against the interests of small firms through its apparent preoccupation with big business and through how the tax system affected small firms.

Despite these challenges, the business owners expressed a reluctance, or unwillingness, to accept outside advice from government or other sources, leading Golby and Johns to remark:

> This constant discussion of financial and labour problems, on the one hand, and the reluctance to explore sources of outside assistance on the other, is probably the key finding in this study. This apparent inconsistency can only be explained by a proper appreciation of the motivation of the owner of the small firm.
>
> (Ibid., p.5)

In discussions of what the business owners valued in running their own firms, the responses reported are familiar. Ideas around independence, close personal relationships and a sense of achievement in overcoming challenges were all cited. Money, while significant to a degree, was relegated in importance behind these personal satisfactions. The responses led Golby and Johns to note the presentation of 'almost the

Smilesian stereotype' (ibid., p.10), contrasting their own industrious-ness, 'craggy independence' and 'a sense of personal responsibility' with the banal existence lived out in large businesses (on the relevance of Samuel Smiles' work in establishing these characteristics, see Mallett and Wapshott, 2020).

Golby and Johns (ibid., p.16) highlight tensions in the accounts offered by the small business owners, contrasting the self-image offered of 'resilient adventurers of today – ingenious, adaptable, quick to solve problems which would baffle the semi-moribund industrial giants' with conservatism in practice. On the matter of finance, the bank manager was typically viewed as the only source of funds, despite the impact of the prevailing economic climate on the availability of funds from traditional sources. Golby and Johns note that the 'whole approach is in obvious contrast to the willingness to take a chance and to back a hunch which was claimed during the earlier discussion about the essen-tial advantages offered by the small business' (ibid., p.22).

With regard to attitudes towards business growth, although most participants indicated a willingness to grow, Golby and Johns express a degree of scepticism around this: 'there seems to be an element of lip service in this response, which is hardly surprising at a time when growth seems to have become almost equivalent to godliness' (ibid., p.19). Against this majority, view was a sizable minority in favour of maintaining the status quo in their firm. Among these owners, tax-ation and other government-imposed constraints were given as reasons. However, Golby and Johns inject a note of caution against over-analysing such responses by adding that:

> the preference for maintaining a comfortable routine and having an easier life also play their part, together with the desire to retain personal contact and control. Only very rarely, did respondents admit openly that they might be afraid to expand.
>
> (Ibid., pp.19–20)

Access to Finance

Matters of finance represented a consistent area of concern for the business owners and was a specified area of research conducted for the Committee. The EAG undertook two reports for the Committee addressing *Financial Facilities for Small Firms* (Lees et al., 1971) and *Problems of the Small Firm in Raising External Finance – The Results of a Sample Survey* (Dunning et al., 1971). Of particular interest to the research report led by Lees was whether a Macmillan-style gap in the provision of finance for small firms remained. Given that access to finance had provided one of the central points of impetus for enterprise policymaking to this date (including leading to the formation of the ICFC, which was now led by Bolton Committee member Lawrence Tindale), this was a central question to the Committee's work. The researchers concluded that 'there is no single major defect in financial facilities for small firms that calls for radical action. In short, there is no "Bolton gap"' (Lees et al., 1971, p.v).

In order to make better sense of this report and its main findings, it is important to recognise the sources of information drawn on by the EAG. While Lees et al. (1971, p.3) explain how published information was used where this was possible, they found that useful information was in short supply. As a result, they recourse to 'a large number of interviews with individual institutions in each of the main types of financial institution'. The study was, therefore, largely a study of organisations providing financial facilities:

> clearing banks; merchant banks; overseas banks transacting UK business; discount houses; finance houses; insurance companies; pension funds; stockbrokers and new issue houses (other than merchant banks); firms specialising in leasing, factoring and export finance; building societies; firms specialising in medium-term finance (including ICFC and relevant subsidies of clearing banks); and firms specialising in finance for technical innovation, including NRDC.
>
> (Ibid., p.1)

Despite the range of institutions involved in the study, 'Very few suggestions were put by the institutions interviewed; there was a general feeling that the difficulties of providing finance for small firms were "facts of life", and that nothing much could be done about them' (ibid., p.41). The report indicates that lenders were discouraged from lending to small firms by perceived shortcomings in the standard of management and an absence of the necessary financial controls. High rates of personal taxation were also identified as a barrier to small firms financing, limiting the amounts available in personal savings to invest in small firms. For its part, the research team identified some further constraints, such as the available interest rates and the charges involved in accessing finance.

Lees et al. do not report small firms as being subjected to deliberate discrimination. Rather, as a result of certain facts of life and unintended consequences, small firms found themselves relatively disadvantaged in relation to financing when compared to large firms. The 'facts of life' were explained in terms of transaction costs and information costs. Transaction costs, which were relatively more expensive for small firms to bear than large, resulted in higher rates for small firms. Greater information costs between lenders and prospective borrowers were such that small firm owners were often uninformed of the available options for finance, and lenders were uninformed about the financial performance and potential of a prospective borrower. Further difficulties stemmed from the unintended consequences of government policy, for instance, with lending ceilings affecting small firms more severely than large firms and taxation policy restricting the availability of internal funding sources to support the growth of small firms. Small firms were also affected by certain conventions operating in the financial institutions that could negatively impact small firms, for instance, being rejected for loans on the assumption they would only want a low rate out of line with the risk, rather than giving them the opportunity to take the loan at an appropriate (higher) rate.

While the report did not identify a gap in available finance for small firms, it nonetheless noted 'the general inadequacy and fragmented nature of the advice and information available to small firms on financial and related matters' (ibid., p.74). In some ways, this connected with the concerns about the quality of management in small firms discussed above. They, therefore, offered suggestions for adjustments that might ease the availability of finance for small firms, including the suggestion of a central agency with two broad functions. These functions would be, firstly, to educate small firms' managers in financial management and how to present their businesses to the financial institutions. Secondly, the proposed agency would focus on providing accountants and solicitors with up-to-date information on sources of finance 'so that they might better advise the small businessman in the increasingly complex environment in which he operates' (ibid., p.74).

The recommendation of a government, or government-backed, agency was the limit of the authors' appetite for government subsidy. The report concludes by noting that:

> we would be opposed to other forms of subsidy to offset relative disadvantages of smallness generally, like higher transaction costs on borrowing. There is no case, on economic grounds, for supporting small firms simply because they are small.
>
> (Ibid., p.75)

Where Lees et al. focused on the institutional aspects of finance, Dunning and colleagues, also at the EAG, presented *Problems of the*

Small Firm in Raising External Finance – The Results of a Sample Survey. In this study, the EAG was tasked with studying both small firms and financial institutions to understand the respective views of these parties on the matter of raising external finance. Attention was also paid to discovering how well-informed small firms were on the different sources of finance available and the basis for their decisions in choosing which particular financial institutions to approach.

Dunning et al. recruited firms that had responded to the Bolton Committee's earlier questionnaire. These firms were selected initially by the Committee as pairs of similar firms that reported having been respectively unsuccessful and successful in applying for finance. Of the 64 pairs of firms approached, Dunning et al. achieved a sample of 19 pairs, and 50 firms overall, to participate in the study. The sample was spread across manufacturing (n = 30) and non-manufacturing (n = 20) firms spread across the Midlands (×6), North East England (×8), North West England (×11), London (×8) and Southern England (×17). Nevertheless, the study was hampered by concerns affecting the quality of the underlying data and interpreting what constituted being 'successful' or 'unsuccessful' in applications for finance, or what amounted to an 'attempt' to secure finance (Ibid., p.3).

One further limitation was identified by the report authors and it is interesting to locate the study in the context of gathering information from small firms:

> it must be said that the tenor of the response from several firms interviewed suggests they volunteered their co-operation primarily to have an opportunity to voice their sense of grievance at some particular government measure which seems to bear on them particularly harshly or unfairly. Although we have tried to ensure as much objectivity as possible, this does raise certain doubts about the representativeness of our survey.
>
> (Ibid., p.4)

In Dunning et al.'s analysis, the successful firms were generally found to be above average when compared to the sample as a whole, for profit/sales ratio and growth performance over recent years. Finance was required in order to expand and there was a clarity of purpose in obtaining the funding. These successful applicants were also characterised as being well informed or well advised on matters of finance and the available sources of finance. The firms that had successfully applied for funding were characterised as not being 'over-ambitious in their requests for finance; on the other hand they were persevering in their attempts to obtain the funds they needed on the most favourable terms' (ibid., p.ix) and able to take the challenging environment in their stride.

In contrast, those firms that had been unsuccessful in their attempts to secure finance during 1968 and 1969, were characterised as being less profitable than the sample as a whole and in search of funding to defend the business or for no particular purpose. These firms were described as 'inclined to complain about both an "availability of funds" and an "information gap"' while experiencing adverse effects from government credit restrictions and fiscal measures (ibid., p.ix). Finally, these unsuccessful firms 'were managerially and financially unsophisticated; nor did they always seem to get the best advice from their accountant or bank manager' and they 'lacked perseverance in seeking for finance, sometimes giving up at the first attempt' (ibid., p.x).

In drawing together their conclusions and presenting their recommendations, the report's authors confirmed the conclusion of their colleagues Lees et al., that there was no single, major defect that needed to be addressed. Rather, there were a number of smaller matters that could be tackled. Dunning et al. (1971, p.x) identified that 'at least for some forms of finance, both a "publicity" and a "knowledge" gap exists' and the case was re-stated for a central agency to educate small firms on sources of finance and how to approach them. Another echo of the report on *Financial Facilities for Small Firms* was the recommendation that 'more might be done to educate accountants, bank managers, insurance brokers, and the like in sources of finance and to encourage these financial intermediaries, both separately and jointly to provide better finance doctoring services' (ibid., p.xi).

Responses of the Committee

The research reports informed Committee discussions. Golby and Johns' study of owner-manager attitudes was discussed with approval. In particular, Tindale is recorded as considering that this report was particularly helpful in providing the Committee with the '"feel" of the people in the small business sector'. He felt this provided a valuable counterbalance to the reliance on statistical data elsewhere in the planned Committee Report (BT262/21/CSF247, TNA).

Other reports, such as that by Hebden and Robinson on the motor trade, were also welcomed as informing the Committee members' understanding of particular sectors in the economy. However, it is worth noting that the Committee agreed that the Automobile Association (AA) should be asked for its unofficial comments on the report before it was published (BT262/21/CSF287, TNA). It was also agreed at the same meeting that the research reports should be sent to the relevant Economic Development Committee (EDC) offices and Government departments 'for unofficial comments'. Nor was the Committee an uncritical recipient of the research reports. Discussing the opening section of Smith's *Small Retailers: Prospects and Policies*, Committee minutes record that it was 'rather confusing and should be rewritten before publication' (BT262/21/CSF247, TNA).

Conclusion

Reviewing the research reports in overview, it is possible to recognise several of the central themes that would shape the Committee's final report and recommendations (discussed in Chapter 7). The challenges of applying generic definitions of size to examine quite different sectors of the economy were apparent and reflected in the comments of the research report authors. However, as the Committee recognised in its final report (1971, p.32), working with more suitable definitions for different sectors could conflict with a need to offer some broader comments on the small firm sector as a whole. Similarly, and unsurprisingly in light of the Committee's own difficulties, the researchers also reported their difficulties accessing information. Despite the general perception ahead of the Committee, that the problems facing the sector were well-understood, the large-scale, cross-sector research effort reveals just how limited understanding of small firms was at this time.

The research reports highlighted the potentially problematic role played by the small firm owners, at least in terms of bringing dynamism to a small firms sector. Findings called into question business owners' level of management skill, access to appropriate advice and their overall ambition for growing their ventures. This points to an important distinction that is drawn out in the Committee's conclusions between the value perceived in small firms and their doubts expressed about their owner-managers. The potential role for small firms as a sector in the economy remains, for instance, providing a seedbed for growing ventures or representing the acorns that grow into oaks, but the owners of the individual firms might not be the people capable of delivering this.

In other words, the role of small firms in the economy and the problems facing them, as set out in the terms of reference, can be seen as two distinct matters. The role of small firms, in terms of their overall economic function, does not necessarily relate to the problems facing the owners of those businesses; the role of firms can be understood as an aggregated understanding of the activity produced by firms employing fewer than 200 people, whereas the problems facing small firms were frequently reported as resting with individual owner-managers. This tension would also emerge in some of the political debate around small firms that we discuss in Chapter 6.

References

Bolton, J.E. (1971). *Committee of inquiry on small firms,* Cmnd. 4811. London: H.M.S.O. (reprint).

Boswell, J. (1973). *The rise and decline of small firms.* London: George Allen & Unwin.

BT262/20/CSF/71, TNA: 15th Committee meeting, 26 November 1969.

BT262/20/CSF77, TNA: 16th Committee meeting, 4 December 1969.

BT262/20/CSF79, TNA: 17th Committee meeting, 11 December 1969.

BT262/20/CSF106, TNA: 20th Committee meeting, 12 February 1970.

BT262/21/CSF247, TNA: 47th Committee meeting, 28 September 1970.

BT262/21/CSF287, TNA: 54th Committee meeting, 25 November 1970.

BT360/9/61a, TNA: The Committee on Small Firms: The Research Programme, Preliminary Report, February 1970.

Davies, J.R. and Kelly, M. (1972). *Small firms in the manufacturing sector.* London: H.M.S.O.

Dunning, J.H. et al./Economists Advisory Group (1971). *Problems of the small firm in raising external finance – the results of a sample survey.* London: H.M.S.O.

Freeman, C. (1971). *The role of small firms in innovation in the UK since 1945.* London: H.M.S.O.

Golby, C.W. and Johns, G. (1971). *Attitude and motivation.* London: H.M.S.O.

Hall, M. (1971). *The small unit in the distributive trades.* London: H.M.S.O.

Hebden, J. and Robinson, R.V.F. (1971). *The small firm in the motor vehicle distribution and repair industry.* London: H.M.S.O.

Hillebrandt, P. (1971). *Small firms in the construction industry.* London: H.M.S.O.

Hollander, E.D. (1967). *The future of small business.* New York: Frederick A. Praeger, Publishers.

Ingham, G.K. (1970). *Size of organization and worker behaviour.* London: Cambridge University Press.

Kaplan, A.D.H. (1948). *Small business: Its place and problems.* New York: Committee for Economic Development / McGraw-Hill Book Company, Inc.

Lees, D. et al./Economists Advisory Group (1971). *Financial facilities for small firms.* London: H.M.S.O.

Lund, P. and Miner, D. (1971). *Three studies on small firms.* London: H.M.S.O.

Mallett, O. and Wapshott, R. (2020). *A history of enterprise policy: Government, small business and entrepreneurship.* New York: Routledge.

Pickering, J.F., Greenwood, J.A. and Hunt, D. (1971). *The small firm in the hotel and catering industry.* London: H.M.S.O.

Radcliffe, C. (1959). *Committee on the working of the monetary system, Report,* Cmnd. 827. London: H.M.S.O.

Research Unit (1972). *A postal questionnaire survey of small firms: Non-financial data, tables, definitions and notes.* London: H.M.S.O.

Smith, A.D. (1971). *Small retailers: Prospects and policies.* London: H.M.S.O.

Tamari, M. (1972). *A postal questionnaire survey of small firms: An analysis of financial data.* London: H.M.S.O.

Todd, D. (1971). *The relative efficiency of small and large firms.* London: H.M.S.O.

Woodward, J. (1965/1980). *Industrial organization: Theory and practice* (2nd edition). Oxford: Oxford University Press.

6 Small Business and Small Government?

Introduction

The Bolton Committee had worked to collect significant amounts of data from and about a broad range of stakeholders. Conducting such a large data collection process necessarily took time and so the evidence was gathered over many months, not to mention the ongoing analysis of the evidence and drafting of the Committee's conclusions. In understanding the production of the Committee's report and the recommendations they advanced (discussed in Chapter 7), it is important to understand the changing political context in which this work was conducted. Most significantly this involved a change in government following the Conservative victory in the General Election of June 1970.

In this chapter, we trace the changing political landscape in which the Committee conducted its work. The Committee was founded under a Labour administration committed to state intervention in industry, but found itself concluding its work and reporting to a Conservative government promising lower taxes, a commitment to free enterprise and less government intervention in industry. We explore the different views provided to the Committee by politicians of the day and consider the implications for the Committee's work.

A Live Debate

As discussed in Chapter 3, the early 1960s had seen an apparent consensus around the role of government and planning in the economy. It was the Conservatives under Macmillan, not a Labour government, that introduced the National Economic Development Council and that set an annual growth target (Meadows, 1978). During the course of the decade, however, this consensus started to show signs of strain. Towards

DOI: 10.4324/9781003119142-6

the end of the 1960s and into the 1970s, commentators were increasingly critical of the levels of government intervention in British industry (Middlemas, 1983).

Writing during Labour's time in office, for example, Broadway (1969, p.10) suggested that government intervention at the time was 'substantially greater than anything imposed upon industry in peace time since the industrial revolution' other than the period after the Second World War, 'when another Labour administration inherited and made full use of a massive apparatus of controls'.

The Bolton Committee were attentive to debates and different perspectives that were being shared outside of its meetings. The archival records include a wide range of newspaper articles, commentaries and press releases on a range of topics that were circulated to Committee members. This material represented an array of views, highlighting again the complexity of what the Committee was faced with. It also highlights the range of stakeholders with an interest in shaping the outcome of the Committee's work, including through debates in the media. This wider reporting and debate about the Committee and its work represents an important component in understanding the political context in which the Committee operated.

For example, an article on *The Small Business and the Economic Climate*, published in the *National Westminster Bank Quarterly Review* in February 1970, was circulated to the Committee with a summary of its key points (BT360/9/83 and BT360/9/83a, TNA). The summary draws out a characterisation of independent but vulnerable small firms facing shortages of capital, information, research, marketing facilities and consultative expertise. The article suggests that large firms should be interested in these businesses as an opportunity to 'replenish their stock of enterprise' but that governments have ignored them, favouring large firms and nationalisation (and at times damaging small firms, for example, through the Selective Employment Tax). However, the article foresaw that small firms would become more important as large companies were increasingly bureaucratic, in contrast to the greater flexibility of small firms, which offered potentially greater rewards for both employees and employers. In this context, the article argued for the benefits of a Small Business Service.

Other articles highlighted for the Committee's attention included those that commented directly on the work of the Committee itself. For example, *The Times* (T342/115, TNA) from 13 August 1970 featured an article on *Whitehall's Paperwork and the Small Businessman*. This article commented specifically on the Central Statistical Office's (CSO) 'note' to the Bolton Committee saying that small firms are not over-burdened by the forms that they send out. The article suggests that: 'The CSO's real achievement with its "note" to the Bolton Committee may in fact be that it represents a blow struck by Whitehall against the common assumption that the Civil Service is a burden on the community.'

Another article in *The Times*, published in December 1970, reported that the Bolton Committee was expected to recommend the setting up of a permanent centre for small firms that would 'carry out research into probems (sic) affecting smaller firms, and put views to the Government' (BT361/15a, TNA). The article noted that, as we discuss below, this was in line with previous Conservative proposals, highlighting the importance of contemporary political debates for the Committee's work.

Meetings with the Government and Civil Servants

To better understand the position of small firms in the economy, and particularly their relations to government, the Committee sought the views of government and opposition politicians, but also of civil servants. Whatever the government policy of the day, it was civil servants who fulfilled an essential role in the implementation of that policy. Gaining an appreciation of how civil servants in departments such as the Board of Trade viewed small firms further enriches our understanding of the context in which the Committee was operating.

An interesting example of such a meeting occurred on 5 March 1970 with senior Civil Servants and the Minister of State from the Board of Trade, Lord Brown. The meeting represented the Committee's first political briefing from the government since its formation in July 1969. The brief for Lord Brown ahead of the meeting indicated that the Committee would benefit from some guidance on the kinds of recommendation that might be 'politically acceptable and administratively workable' (BT360/10/25, TNA). In a paper prepared for Committee members, the Secretariat explained that the meeting would have two parts, the first with the civil servants and the Minister, the second with the Minister alone. The arrangement was made in this way because the views of officials and the Minister were said to differ on a range of topics, and the Minister might speak more openly in a separate meeting. Further background information was provided such as the Minister's strong support for a national consultancy grant scheme for small firms and members were informed that 'There will, therefore, be some disappointment if the Committee oppose the idea' (BT360/10/ 25, TNA).

At the meeting, the Board of Trade officials explained that the Committee had been established largely because the department recognised a need for understanding the problems encountered by small firms. Moreover, a degree of ignorance might have characterised the Board of Trade position on small firms, but this was not a reflection of any particular antagonism. It was explained further that, typically, the Board of Trade had interacted with trade associations or larger businesses, and it appeared that small firms had been affected by priorities set without them in mind, for instance, the focus on rationalisation (BT262/20/CSF121, TNA).

Despite not having a specific policy focus on small firms in the way that existed in the United States with its Small Business Administration, and although not forming part of an overall 'philosophy' on small firms, officials explained that ministries still had regard for the particular problems facing small firms. The Board of Trade, for instance, provided subsidies in the region of £11m annually to the benefit of small firms, such as the subsidy to the British Productivity Council. According to the minutes, the representatives went on to explain how 'the American Government had framed its small firm policy largely to take account of the pressure groups which did not operate for Britain' (BT262/20/CSF121, TNA).

Lord Brown also defended the role of government in relation to small firms. According to the record of the meeting (BT262/20/CSF121, TNA), Lord Brown attributed much of the apparent displeasure of small firms with the Labour government to their misunderstanding of policies and it 'had at its root a political autagonism (sic) towards the Labour Government'. Responding to Bolton's comment on the psychological harm done to small businesses owing to ignorance of the rules governing shortfall provisions contained in the 1965 Finance Act, Lord Brown is recorded as pointing out that the Inland Revenue had adopted a relatively liberal stance. Nevertheless, he recounted a lunch he had attended at which most of the business people present remained ignorant of changes in the 1969 Finance Act that had removed limits on directors' salaries.

The general tone of the Minister's assessment of small firms continued in a similar vein. The minutes record Lord Brown's view on the availability of financing for small firms as being:

> that many businessmen claimed that the credit squeeze was preventing their expansion. In many instances, however, this was an alibi. The real reason why many firms did not expand was an irrational fear by the owner that he would lose control through dilution of capital [although he also recognised that company floatation was very expensive].

On the matter of a national consultancy grants scheme, Lord Brown explained how he had introduced the idea to help overcome management problems in British industry. The scheme had been pilot tested in Bristol and Glasgow, with assessments being that the exercise had proven successful. Although the consultancy profession, which was already growing at 10% per year, had initially expressed some scepticism about the industry's capacity to support the additional demand generated by such a scheme, Lord Brown indicated that the profession was now less sceptical about how the scheme might be delivered. For their part, the Committee was yet to be convinced either way about such a scheme, according to comments attributed to Bolton (BT262/20/CSF121, TNA).

The following week, the Committee hosted representatives from the Labour Party Economics Group (BT360/11/CSF133, TNA). Perhaps unsurprisingly, the representatives echoed Lord Brown's tone. Government measures were regarded as generally not being significantly detrimental to small businesses. Discussion of credit policy reflected that while official ceilings on bank credit were not ideal, it was suggested that much of the difficulty reported by small firms in accessing credit was on the grounds of commercial assessments by the banks rather than the 'credit squeeze' effects of government policy. Indeed, the meeting record reflects a view that banks liked to use the credit squeeze as an excuse. It was also noted that 'the quality of the advice given by bankers and accountants, though it was the best available, was often very bad.' Discussing how small firms could be represented in government, sentiment appeared to be in favour of having a Minister with overall responsibility, 'a new agency outside the existing Departments and without a responsible minister would be quite ineffectual.' (BT360/11/CSF133, TNA).

The Conservative Opposition

The Committee also took note of the views of Conservative MPs from the official opposition, who were vocal on small firms and were critical of the prior political consensus on planning in matters of industry (Middlemas, 1983; Gamble, 1974). Former member of the Shadow Cabinet and now backbencher, following his infamous 'Rivers of Blood' speech on immigration, Enoch Powell was very vocal in setting out his views on state neutrality in matters of industry and commerce. Powell argued for leaving markets to decide the optimal size for businesses; his position against state intervention, as benefitting the interests of large firms, positioned him as the voice of small capital (Gamble, 1974). In a speech to the Retail Credit Federation, a copy of which was held by the Committee, Powell set out his belief that 'Government and the law ought to be as nearly as possible neutral in the matter of the size of businesses.'

Powell took aim directly at the Bolton Committee, describing Bolton's comments about helping small businesses to grow more quickly as 'preposterous'. He explained:

> If small businesses (whatever that means) grow (whatever that means) more quickly, it must mean that other businesses grow more slowly, for the rate at which as businesses together grow is the rate of increase of the labour force or the gross national product or whatever other criterion is being used. But no one has any right to assume that small businesses ought to be growing more quickly and larger businesses less quickly.
>
> BT360/9/74a, TNA

Another influential figure was Keith Joseph, spokesperson on Trade and a key shaper of Conservative policy. Joseph was considered 'a guru of the competitive market economy' (Halcrow, 1989: 4; Young, 1990) and an important influence on the intellectual underpinning of Thatcherism (Morris, 1991). He embodied the Conservative position in favour of free markets and had accused the Labour government of hostility towards small firms, not least when he provided the foreword to the Conservative Political Centre pamphlet *Acorns to Oaks* (Weatherill and Cope, 1969, p.6).

In Parliament, Joseph moved to criticise the government's handling of the Industrial Reorganisation Corporation (IRC) and the scope of powers granted to it. He told the House:

> When we are the Government, if the I.R.C. is still performing a useful function, we shall reconsider the width of its powers very carefully. A facilitating I.R.C.—that is, facilitating the market mechanism—is one thing and may be useful. A fighting I.R.C. is another animal altogether, because it uses the taxpayer's purse to back its judgment on what, in almost every case, can only be a hypothetical and marginal difference in national interest.
>
> HC Deb, 8 July 1968

The Committee received briefing notes for the meeting with Joseph that highlighted the shift in Conservative Party opinion on a 'Small Business Development Bureau' (BT360/11/24, TNA). While the Party's

1966 manifesto had promised to 'Set up a Small Business Development Bureau to help small firms start and grow' and Joseph had repeated the pledge in his foreword to *Acorns to Oaks* that a Conservative government would introduce such an office, Press reports from Spring 1970 had indicated that the idea was being revisited. In what was presented as a 'major change in Conservative Party thinking on the working of a small business development agency', the plans for a 'bureau' modelled on the United States' Small Business Administration were to be revisited amid fears that 'calling the organisation a "bureau" might be regarded by some as symptomatic of thoughts on bureaucracy and further Government interference in industry' (Financial Times, 13 March 1970, p.12). The article reported that plans would be presented to Shadow Cabinet for scaling back a US-style Small Business Administration in favour of an information and development support function delivered through Small Business Centres.

The Committee's files also contain a number of Press releases and newspaper cuttings reporting Joseph's recent speeches. In one such address to the West Midlands Young Conservative Conference in February 1970, Joseph placed an emphasis on free enterprise and a dynamic economy in which small firms would play an important role for social as well as economic reasons:

> Socially, we want as many men and women as possible to have the fulfilment and independence that comes from building a small or medium-sized business ... Industrially, small businesses are the broad, resilient base on which the economy is built.
>
> BT360/11/24

In an article from the Daily Telegraph (6 April 1970), Conservative MP John Biffen explored his party's position on free enterprise, as expounded by Joseph. As well as recognising the significant role attributed to Joseph in setting out the Conservative position on free enterprise, Biffen highlights Joseph's criticism of 'public interference with private industry' and assumptions that 'a planned collusion between Whitehall and selected businessmen is the best way to promote wealth and discharge the social obligations of a modern industrial society' (BT360/11/24, TNA).

Heading into the meeting with Joseph, therefore, the Committee members could be under no illusions as to the divisions in British politics during the run-up to the June 1970 election. The Government of the day was in favour of further planning in the economy and supporting small businesses through consultancy grants. The opposition, and possible future government, was setting itself firmly against what it saw as government extending its remit into areas best left to free enterprise.

Meeting the Committee in April 1970, the records show that Joseph played down a role for active government support. While emphasising small firms' 'important contribution in moral and libertarian terms to the quality of life', Joseph nonetheless outlined opposition to government subsidy of finance or consultancy services to support these businesses (BT360/11/33, TNA; also BT360/6/9, TNA). In line with a Conservative shift in focus from market failure to addressing government failure, Joseph emphasised relieving the damage caused by the unforeseen consequences of government actions through greater foresight and consultation, rather than expending money to remedy such harms after the fact. Joseph argued that, to achieve this end, small firms needed a strong voice outside government as well as within government, where a Junior Minister could take on responsibility for acting as a focal point for small business interests.

In the midst of its data gathering and its efforts to formulate recommendations against its terms of reference, the Committee was working against a diverging political background and the beginning of the end of a political consensus around the role of government in the economy and industry. The incumbent Labour government was seemingly content to continue along the lines of government planning, while the Conservative opposition was setting itself in favour of smaller government and free markets. These divisions were to become clearer and carry implications for the Committee, during and following the 1970 General Election.

General Election 1970

The Labour government had presided over a poor economy for much of 1966–1970, leading to abandoned policy pledges, industrial disputes and by-election losses. There were also divisions within the Labour Party over areas of socially liberalising reforms that it had introduced such as legalising homosexuality. However, Wilson's government saw some recovery in the latter part of 1969. The balance of payments figures showed improvement, along with the government's rating in the polls. The Labour manifesto *Now Britain's Strong – Let's Make It Great To Live In* (see Craig, 1990, p.132), played on the improving economy and the important role for planning. It warned of 'a return to the Tory free-for-all' under which 'people become the victims of economic forces they cannot control.' Within the Labour vision, however, there appeared to be no mention of small firms.

In contrast, the Conservatives criticised the effects of government bureaucracy on industry and sought to take on the mantle of 'modernisation'. Their proposal to the electorate included a freer economy but a stronger state in areas such as law and order. Their manifesto also included comments addressing how small businesses would benefit from its general approach to smaller government, including making specific mention of the Bolton Report:

> Small businesses have had a raw deal from Labour. They have had to suffer higher and more complicated taxes, and waste more time filling up forms. Our policies for reducing taxation and reducing government interference in industry will reduce the heavy burdens on the small firm. We will decide the best method of providing advice and encouragement for small businesses in the light of the Bolton Report.
>
> *A Better Tomorrow;* see Craig, 1990, p.120

For its part, the Liberal manifesto *What a Life!* made a pitch against the established interests in politics, and in the economy that favoured 'bigness'. 'The whole "System" conspires against the individual' while 'Big business tycoons and trade union bosses have a powerful say in British politics' through their respective patronage of the establishment Conservative and Labour parties. Setting out their case to the 'ordinary people' that Liberal MPs would represent, the small business is highlighted as a Liberal concern.

Highlighting the rates of small business failure over recent years, the manifesto points to policies such as the selective employment tax, the burdens of bureaucracy and the effects of the credit squeeze on small firms. The problems created by these hurdles facing small and medium-sized firms were of national importance given the contribution made by these businesses to employment, GNP and exports (see Craig, 1990, p.156).

The General Election campaign appeared to be going well for the Labour Party. However, its progress was derailed by an unexpected balance of payments deficit announced for May, followed by deflationary measures in response. These measures antagonised trade unions and risked alienating Labour-voting workers. Further, as Dorey (2013, p.86) notes, the party 'repeatedly struggled to secure the confidence of either domestic or international business communities, almost regardless of the measures it took to tackle Britain's serious economic problems'. Then, during election week itself, the incumbent government suffered a further setback when the England football team was knocked out of the World Cup (Denver and Garnett, 2014).

For Butler (1995, p.26), 'Labour was punished for four years of economic uncertainty' and victory for Heath's Conservative Party, returned with a 30-seat majority, was 'the reward for being an acceptable alternative to a government that had been through troubled times' (Butler, 1995, p.26).

The New Conservative Government

In his first Conference speech as Prime Minister, Conservative leader Edward Heath set out his new government's agenda. In addition to addressing at some length questions of Britain's role in the international community, he addressed domestic matters (Heath, 1970). Heath explained that his government would reshape the scale of government and be altogether less interventionist than his Labour predecessors. In Parliament, this vision was mapped out in a series of White Papers. The Heath government presented its agenda for reorganising central government (Cmnd. 4506) and areas of public spending (Cmnd. 4516, Cmnd. 4515).

As part of 'reshaping' government, an emphasis was placed on reducing its scope and scale, including the role it played in industry. The IRC, with its interventionist remit to strengthen the competitiveness of British industry, was to be wound-up and the grant to the British Productivity Council would be phased out (Cmnd. 4515; Pass, 1971). In this spirit of leaner government, the newly formed Department of Trade and Industry was specifically tasked with reviewing existing services provided to assist industry. The task of reviewing the 'size and methods' (Cmnd. 4506, p.8) of these services, was to examine the cost-effectiveness and success in achieving its goals. The scope of this review was to explicitly include 'export promotion services, export credits, a wide range of advisory services notably for small and medium-sized firms' (Cmnd. 4506, p.9).

Meanwhile, at the time when the Bolton Committee was fielding complaints about the tax burdens on small firms, the new government was committed to cutting corporation tax. As it was presented, the planned phasing out of the investment grants scheme would see those savings to government returned to industry through tax allowances on investment and reductions in corporation tax. Further, the planned reduction in the rate of Corporation Tax, by 2½ percentage points, was aimed to provide:

> a significant stimulus to industry, including small but expanding businesses. It will also provide an immediate and desirable addition

to company liquidity. A Bill will be introduced without delay to amend the provisions of the Finance Act 1970 accordingly.

(Cmnd. 4516, p.3)

The Chancellor's proposals on Public Expenditure and Taxation contained in Cmnd. 4515 and Cmnd. 4516 were debated in Parliament the following week. The new Secretary of State for Trade and Industry and President of the Board of Trade was John Davies, the former head of the CBI who had been instrumental in the establishment of the Bolton Committee and was elected to Parliament in June 1970. Davies emphasised the new government's belief that:

> the need to encourage the individual to have a greater and not a lesser say in the conduct of his life is now an essential. National decadence is the consequence of treating us all, the whole country, as though we were lame ducks ... The vast majority lives and thrives in a bracing climate and not in a soft, sodden morass of subsidised incompetence.

HC Deb, 4 November 1970

The change of government and the new government's radically different approach, at least in terms of how it set out its initial agenda, represented a significantly different context for the Bolton Committee. This change and its implications are apparent in the recorded Committee meetings. In May 1970, John Bolton spoke in favour of a national scheme of grants to support consultancy in small businesses (BT262/20/CSF169, TNA) although other committee members, notably Tew, seem to have been less convinced by the same evidence (BT262/20/CSF176, TNA; BT262/71, TNA). Later that year, in early November and following the recent statements of intent from the Government, Bolton indicated that he was no longer inclined to support a national system of consultancy grants (BT262/21/CSF273, TNA).

A document from the Committee Secretariat outlining the views of the Committee to aid re-drafting of the chapter on Advisory Services noted that, unlike the former Labour government:

> The Conservative Administration has not made any sympathetic noises' regarding subsidised consultancy for small firms. It was also noted that the new government was 'committed to a philosophy of reducing Government intervention and expenditure' and further emphasised the phasing out of support for the BPC and consideration being given to similar spending reductions

(BT360/13/CSF270, TNA)

In the area of taxation, the Committee was concerned to share its views with the Minister for Industry. The Committee wrote to John Eden in January 1971 sharing its agreed recommendations to date so that they might be considered ahead of Budget planning, given that the Committee's full report would arrive with Ministers too late for these views to be considered. The nine interim recommendations touched on shortfall assessments, treatment of interest against income tax and abolishing Selective Employment Tax, alongside recommending changes on estate duty, capital gains and retirement provisions. The final Report makes explicit reference to this letter, and in fact reproduces it (1971, p.231–234), explaining that some of the Committee's intended recommendations on taxation had been omitted from the Report because the 1971 Finance Act had covered these matters. This perhaps indicates one of the challenges faced by the Committee when working against a changing political backdrop: the chance that its conclusions and recommendations would be outstripped by events.

Conclusion

In previous chapters, we have commented on the challenges facing the Committee in building the foundation of knowledge required to address the terms of reference. In addition to building understanding of the situation for small firms in the economy, the Committee was also tasked with developing recommendations for government. It is essential, therefore, to recognise that the Committee was working within a dynamic political context, reflecting significant political changes as the consensus of the past began to break apart and the major parties' positions diverged at the end of the 1960s and through the 1970 General Election.

Working for some eight months without a particular steer from the Labour government on what might be 'politically acceptable and administratively workable' (BT360/10/25, TNA), the Committee later had to consider the implications of a new, Conservative government with a radically different approach to industry and philosophy on the role of government. The Committee had been convened by a Labour government still committed to government intervention in matters of industry. The Committee would, however, complete the final year of its inquiry and report to a Conservative Government espousing views on smaller and less interventionist government. In Chapter 7 we turn our focus to the production of the Committee's final report and recommendations and their reception by the Conservative Government.

References

Broadway, F. (1969). *State intervention in British industry 1964–68*. London: Kaye & Ward.

BT262/20/CSF121, TNA: 22nd Committee meeting, 5 March 1970.

BT262/20/CSF169, TNA: 31st Committee meeting, 7 May 1970.

BT262/20/CSF176, TNA: 32nd Committee meeting, 14 May 1970.

BT262/21/CSF273, TNA: 52nd Committee meeting, 11 November 1970.

BT262/71, TNA: Individuals (submissions).

BT360/6/9, TNA: Extracts from the Budget Debate, 17 April 1969.

BT360/9/74a, TNA: 'The small business: The ideal is not State aid but State neutrality'. Press notice of speech to Retail Credit Federation, 24 September 1969.

BT360/9/83, TNA: Summary of *'The small business and the economic climate'* for Committee members, 23 February 1970.

BT360/9/83a, TNA: Hollowood, L.B., *'The small business and the economic climate'*. National Westminster Bank Quarterly Review, February 1970.

BT360/10/25, TNA: Meeting with Small Firms Committee, Brief for Lord Brown, 5 March 1970.

BT360/11/24, TNA: Briefing notes for the Committee ahead of meeting Sir Keith Joseph (including Press release of a recent speech by Joseph and Press comment from John Biffen, MP).

BT360/11/33, TNA: Meeting with Sir Keith Joseph, 9 April 1970.

BT360/11/CSF133, TNA: Note of a meeting with Labour Party Economics Group, 12 March 1970.

Butler, D. (1995). *British General Elections since 1945* (2nd edition). Oxford: Blackwell, Oxford (Institute of Contemporary British History).

Cmnd. 4506. (1970). *The reorganisation of central government*. Presented to Parliament by the Prime Minister and Minister for the Civil Service.

Cmnd. 4515. (1970). *New policies for public spending*. Presented to Parliament by the Chancellor of the Exchequer.

Cmnd. 4516. (1970). *Investment incentives*. Presented to Parliament by the Chancellor of the Exchequer and the Secretary of State for Trade and Industry.

Craig, F.W.S. (1990). *British general election manifestos 1959–1987* (3rd edition). Aldershot: Parliamentary Research Services, Dartmouth (publisher). *A better tomorrow* (Conservative Party, 1970); *Now Britain's strong – let's make it great to live in* (Labour Party, 1970); *What a life!* (Liberal Party, 1970).

Denver, D. and Garnett, M. (2014). *British general elections since 1964: Diversity, dealignment, and disillusion*. Oxford: Oxford University Press.

Dorey, P. (2013). The fall of the Wilson Government, 1970. In: T. Heppell and K. Theakston (eds.) *How Labour governments fall*. London: Palgrave Macmillan, pp.83–112.

Financial Times (1970). 'Tories change plan to help small businesses', Ray Spencer, 13 March.

Gamble, A. (1974). *The conservative nation.* London and New York: Routledge & Kegan Paul.

Halcrow, M. (1989). *Keith Joseph: A single mind.* London: Macmillan.

HC Deb (1968). vol.768 col.67, Sir Keith Joseph MP, 8 July.

HC Deb (1970). vol.805 col.1212, John Davies MP, 4 November.

Heath, E. (1970). Party leader's speech. Speech reproduced at URL: www.britishpoliticalspeech.org/speech-archive.htm?speech=117. Accessed 1 May 2021.

Meadows, P. (1978). Planning. In: F.T. Blackaby (ed.) *British economic policy 1960–1974.* Cambridge: Cambridge University Press, pp.402–417.

Middlemas, K. (1983). *Industry, unions and government: Twenty-one years of NEDC.* Macmillan Press Ltd, London and Basingstoke: National Economic Development Council.

Morris, P. (1991). Freeing the spirit of enterprise: The genesis and development of the concept of enterprise culture. In: R. Keat and N. Abercrombie (eds.) *Enterprise culture.* London: Routledge, pp.21–37.

Pass, C. (1971). The Industrial Reorganisation Corporation – A positive approach to the structure of industry. *Long range planning* (September 1971), p.63–70.

The Times (1970). 'Smaller businesses centre may be set up', George Clark, 9 December, BT361/15a, TNA.

The Times (1970). *Whitehall's paperwork and the small businessman,* 13 August, T342/115, TNA.

Weatherill, B. and Cope, J. (1969). *Acorns to Oaks: A policy for small business.* London: Conservative Political Centre.

Young, D. (1990). *The enterprise years: A businessman in the Cabinet.* London: Headline Book Publishing.

7 Recommending the Future of Enterprise Policy

A Less than Dramatic Response

Introduction

Having conducted a major and multifaceted study into small firms in the UK, the Committee came to finalise its report and present its recommendations. The work of the Committee had, contrary to initial expectations, proven to be a substantial undertaking. It had conducted its own large-scale questionnaire, received a wide range of views in submissions of evidence from over 480 stakeholders, commissioned 18 research reports and made fact-finding visits around the UK and abroad. Further, this work was conducted on a topic that revealed itself to be much less well-understood than previously appreciated, and into a small firms 'sector' characterised by striking diversity and heterogeneity.

As the work neared completion, the Committee members had to make sense of the information they had gathered and present a cohesive report with recommendations. In this chapter we explore some of the ongoing discussions among Committee members that led to the final report. We focus primarily on the Committee's recommendations and conclude with an overview of how they were received by government and the civil service, in addition to the reactions of commentators and stakeholders more generally.

Discussing Matters to a Conclusion

Having embarked on their landmark data collection exercise, the Committee members were faced with the challenge of analysing and interpreting the data. The Committee Secretariat provided signifi-cant assistance in preparing and collating materials, for example pro-ducing papers that acted as thematic summaries of the data and of the submissions received, on which the Committee could then pass

DOI: 10.4324/9781003119142-7

comment. The subsequent discussions revealed the high degrees of subjectivity involved in coming to terms with understanding the mixed picture presented in the evidence.

Five months into the committee process, minutes record that Tew had 'felt that Committee members had not thrashed out their views sufficiently on the subjects to be considered' (BT262/20/CSF77, TNA). He seems to have had cause to make a similar complaint in March 1970, with Committee minutes noting that 'an important problem was that the Committee had not debated the most important issues to a conclusion' (BT262/20/CSF142, TNA). By February 1971, lack of clear agreement was delaying the write up of the final report, even as the Committee grew concerned about hitting its further-revised, June 1971 deadline (BT262/21/CSF336, TNA).

Working with a mass of diverse submissions presented challenges in making sense of the evidence and claims submitted to the Committee. The heterogeneity of the small firm sector was apparent in the views expressed both from within the sector and by other stakeholders, making it difficult to distil definitive views (BT262/21/CSF347, TNA). Although it was often difficult, if not impossible, to verify the claims expressed by individual owners of small firms, the Committee recognised how submissions from other stakeholders should also be treated with caution.

Within this context, determining a clear position on specific questions such as whether small firms paid workers more or less than large firms resisted easy resolution (BT262/21/CSF333, TNA). In this case, the survey responses (Research Unit, 1972) provided a range of responses from among small firm respondents. Wage rates compared with large firms in manufacturing were reported as being lower (6%), about the same (51.1%) and higher (18.4%) with the remainder (24.5%) not knowing or not stating. In non-manufacturing it was lower (3.2%), about the same (40.5%), higher (11.6%), with 44.7% not knowing or not stating, albeit with some further differences in response among sectors.

The difficulties of grappling with the information obtained in evidence were not eased by small firms generally lacking a representative voice to speak authoritatively on their behalf. The final report viewed this as part of the problem facing governments and policymakers and apportioned fault to business owners:

> We believe that the apparent indifference and certainly the ignorance of successive governments about small firms is in large part the fault of small business; though the recent formation of the Smaller Businesses Association and the Smaller Firms Council of

the CBI has improved matters, even they often speak with a divided
voice on matters of common concern.

(Bolton Report, 1971, p.93)

In such comments, the Committee might have been reflecting the dominant modes of industrial policy at the time, with large businesses and
industrial constituencies capable of influencing peak organisations and
seeking to offer a single voice to government. Yet, the concerns also
point to the challenges of trying to manage effective industry engagement with the large number of heterogeneous businesses grouped
together by efforts to define small firms as a cohesive sector.

An underlying debate, and a consistent topic of consideration for the
Committee, concerned the question of concentration in the economy,
squeezing opportunities for small firms to compete. Research Director
Graham Bannock, in a book published in 1971 (*The Juggernauts*),
reflects on some of these concerns when discussing the downsides of
'the age of the big corporation'. Bannock argues that dominance in an
economy of the giant corporations was detrimental to market competition, diminished consumer choice and could constrain innovation.

Committee minutes indicate that Tindale, on the other hand,
appeared generally comfortable with concentration, for example as
lower transportation costs had enabled manufacturing to shift from
regional bases to a national economy. If these changes brought about
the demise of inefficient small firms then this was unimportant, what
mattered were opportunities for small businesses to enter markets and
compete (BT262/21/265, TNA). Moreover, as Tew highlighted, short
of clear evidence that small firms had been harmed by mergers of
large firms, the Committee could not recommend greater scrutiny, for
example by the Monopolies Commission (BT262/21/320, TNA).

Uncertainty and disagreement also characterised consideration of
more specific issues in the Committee. Committee members possessed
a diverse range of experience and expertise and they brought this
to bear in deliberations of the evidence. This can be seen in debates
around small firms' access to finance. The initial Committee paper
written by the Secretariat on the topic of access to finance (BT360/
10/124, TNA) brought together a range of evidence and submissions
received and emphasised the difficulties for small firms in retaining of
profits for internal financing and their reliance on bank overdrafts. It
highlighted the Macmillan gap in small firms' difficulties in accessing
finance and stated that this finding had been reinforced by the 1959
Report of the Committee on the Working of the Monetary System
(Radcliffe, 1959).

Bolton, who had personally invested in Solartron and secured further investment for the business (Thomson, 2016), led a Committee discussion on how the range of investors for small firms might be increased, for instance via an over-the-counter share scheme. The minutes of the meeting record a detailed objection from Tindale, Director of the Industrial and Commercial Finance Corporation, an organisation originally set up to address small firms' challenges in accessing finance. Tindale's position was that there was no market for such investments because owners of shares could not easily sell their stock. Moreover, the City had shown little enthusiasm for this type of scheme and the lack of interest from the Stock Exchange in establishing such a vehicle told its own story. According to the minutes, Tindale explained that, rather than thinking of small firms as a body worth 1/6 gross national product (GNP), it was rather a list of investments of unknown quality (BT262/20/CSF201, TNA). Ultimately, no institutional gap in finance provision was identified in the Committee's report and this was reflected in the recommendations (discussed below).

Despite the difficulties inherent in the task of understanding the role of small firms in the economy, the services available to them and the problems they encounter, the Committee worked to produce a coherent report and a significant list of recommendations. Although, as we shall see, the recommendations and the report informing them were subject to certain criticisms, it is nevertheless appropriate to re-emphasise the scale and novelty of the task undertaken by the Committee.

The Committee's Report

The final report of the Bolton Committee covered almost 450 pages and featured around 60 recommendations, relating to nearly every area examined by the Committee. It was divided into two sections. Part One of the report (Chapters 1–7) was drafted by the Research Unit. Part Two (Chapters 8–19) was drafted by the Secretariat and focused on identifying areas of particular concern for small firms.

The first part of the report presented the factual picture of small firms in the UK based on the Committee's inquiries. Framed as presenting an economic analysis of small firms' principal characteristics and their past and present roles in the economy, the report provides an overview of the field as the Committee had found it. In presenting this analysis, the Committee first discussed the definitional challenges it had to face associated with the 200 employee criterion provided in the terms of reference. To overcome the inadequacies of categorising firms across the economy with a single measure, the Committee considered three characteristics that might help explain the particular problems of small firms as compared to larger firms. The Committee held that small firms had a relatively small market share, were managed by their owners without recourse to formal management structures and that the owner-manager enjoyed sufficient control to take the major decisions for the firm, as opposed to being part of a larger venture. These characteristics represented the Committee's 'economic' definition of small firms, but the Committee accepted that for practical purposes a 'statistical' definition had been adopted.

Without sufficiently detailed business population statistics to adopt their more detailed economic definition, the Committee largely worked with statistical definitions, adjusted for industry and based on a combination of existing statistics and estimates from the Research Unit. For example, in Manufacturing the statistical definition was set at 200 employees or less, in Construction the figure was set at 25 employees or less and in Road Transport five vehicles or less (see p.3). The Committee's reservations about defining small firms are expressed in the report, noting for instance that small firms fulfilled a variety of roles in the economy rather than 'the' role set out in the terms of reference. Nevertheless, the Committee also explained that, for the sake of a readable document, some very complex matters were dealt with in somewhat general terms. The tension identified by the Committee, between presenting small firms in sufficient detail to appreciate nuances among them, while also treating them as a recognisable group, has been a persistent feature in UK enterprise policy, often being resolved in favour of the latter position.

Part One of the report concludes with a chapter on the *Causes of the Decline in the Small Firm Sector* which draws out the long-term pattern of decline of small firms in the economy. In common with other nations, small firms in the UK were making a declining contribution to national output and employment. The total number of small firms in the economy was in decline and output from small manufacturers between 1958 and 1963 was stagnant while total manufacturing output increased significantly. Although representing a complex picture, the Committee identified 'an increasingly hostile environment for the small firm' (1971, p.75).

Part Two of the report is focused on a more detailed analysis of particular topics explored through the Committee and the implications for policy. Chapters discuss topics including *Organisation in Government, Management skills and advisory services* and *Sources of finance*, each presenting a series of policy recommendations. The report concludes with Chapter 19, drawing together the *Conclusions and summary of recommendations.*

This structure left an important question in terms of how the two parts of the report would fit together. Part One, with its 'dismal story' (BT262/21/CSF365, TNA), indicated a process of decline in small firm numbers that jarred with the Committee's recommendations against positive discrimination by government to support these firms in Part Two. Discussing this situation when drafting the report, the Committee acknowledged that their assessment of the future prospects for small firms, that the decline would level off, was not based on the evidence presented in Part One. The information on business numbers that had informed the Committee's work was acknowledged to be several years out of date and definitive judgments were not possible (BT262/21/ CSF365, TNA). In the report, this was reconciled by the Committee acknowledging the decline in the numbers of small firms, their share of output and employment but noting that this reflected structural changes, which were necessarily slow, and that small firms would remain a significant part of the economy into the future.

The report emphasised the importance of small firms to the national economy in terms of contribution to GNP and employment. It also offered a view of small firms that contrasted with their portrayal as throwbacks or laggards. Instead, the Committee explained the lower output per person in small firms, compared to large, as reflecting the labour-intensive sectors in which small firms tend to operate and the make-up of the small firms' labour force. Taking into account the better return on capital employed in small firms, the Committee concluded that '… there is no ground for asserting either that as a group large firms are more efficient than small in their use of total resources, or the reverse' (Bolton, 1971, p.342). Nevertheless, the Committee concluded that, as a group, small firms were in decline. Although similar trends were observed in other rich countries, 'the process appears to have gone further in the United Kingdom than elsewhere' (ibid.).

Despite the wider economic changes to which the small firms were subject, the Committee argued that the 'contribution of small businessmen to the vitality of society' (ibid.) and the sector as a whole would remain, owing to their dynamic and adaptable characteristics. Small firms were regarded as serving eight important functions, benefitting the health of the economy:

1 Providing an outlet for enterprising people who were unsuited, or unattracted, to working in a large organisation.
2 Representing the most efficient size of organisation in certain industries and trades.

3   Operating as suppliers of parts or sub-assemblies to larger organisations, achieving lower costs than the larger businesses were able to achieve.

4   Serving niche markets that larger businesses considered uneconomic to serve, contributing to the variety available in the economy more generally.

5   Offering a check on monopoly and inefficiency of large businesses through actual, or potential, competition.

6   Innovating products, services and techniques.

7   As a sector, small firms were held to represent the 'traditional breeding ground for new industries' (ibid., p.343).

8   Small firms represent an entry point for the expression of entrepreneurial talents and the 'the seedbed from which new large companies will grow to challenge and stimulate the established leaders of industry' (ibid.).

It was this eighth function that the Committee considered as perhaps the most important function of all. In formulating recommendations, the Committee's guiding view was that any justification for government intervention on behalf of small firms would need to rest on their national economic contribution. It represents an interesting framing of the small firm sector, given some of the prevailing attitudes expressed about small firms at the time and the portrayal of small business owners as unsophisticated in matters such as finance. Despite the limitations of small firms when viewed as individual businesses, as a sector fulfilling an economic function the Committee presented them as performing a vital role.

Recommendations for Government Action

The Committee provided comment on the wide range of issues they had examined. Among the topics subject to the most recommendations were those of form filling and taxation. In respect of form filling, government departments were implored to consider the time required to complete a statistical request and to be mindful of the costs placed on small firm participants. On matters of taxation, although acknowledging that the government had addressed several areas of complaint raised during the inquiry, the Committee considered that there remained much to be done in the specific details of legislation and creating an overall tax environment that incentivised entrepreneurial endeavour in industry.

The report resisted recommending discrimination in favour of small firms while setting out the necessity for government to maintain conditions in which small firms could compete effectively (ibid., p.344). To achieve this, the government would need to ensure the health of the general economic climate such that small firms would benefit from rising prosperity. The government should be careful to avoid taxation policies that served to disincentivise small firms and it should take action to promote fair competition. Finally, the government should see to it that small firms receive equal treatment under policy and legislation.

The recommendations regarding equal treatment, in many ways, reveal the underlying theme of the Committee's report. The Committee was clear in its view that governments, both Conservative and Labour, had displayed shortcomings in respect of small firms. Nevertheless, and in acknowledged contrast with many of the small firms and small firm advocates who had submitted evidence, the Committee concluded that governments and civil servants were not actively seeking opportunities to hinder and dismantle the small firm sector. Developing this point, the Committee identified that 'Our complaint against Government is simply that the interests of small firms are neglected because it is nobody's job to consider them' (ibid., p.345).

A Small Firms Division

The Committee's central recommendation was for a Small Firms Division, within the Department of Trade and Industry (DTI) and with a DTI Minister charged with overseeing the Division's work. This carried echoes of the Conservative Party's election manifesto pledge in 1966 to create a small firms development bureau, and in 1970 to 'decide the best way of providing advice and encouragement for small businesses in the light of the Bolton Report' (see Craig, 1990).

The Division was to be tasked with collaborating with other government departments to build an understanding of small firms in the economy, now and in the future, based on appropriate research data. This focus on building understanding was despite the Committee's own remit and the two years it had spent seeking to fulfil it, including the largest UK exercise in data collection and analysis of small firms. Two areas were identified by the Committee as priorities for the new Division, namely examining the effect on small firms of entering the European Economic Community (EEC) and considering the impacts of government procurement policies. Moreover, other departments with responsibility for matters relating to trade or industry should allocate to an official the responsibility of overseeing the department's policy towards small firms and liaising with the Small Firms Division.

Creating a new Division within the DTI was to recommend a significant change in the relationship between government and those businesses defined as 'small' under the Committee's terms of reference. Such a recommendation would put small firms on a similar footing to sector interests represented by the Economic Development Committees, with a recognised relationship to government. Through its work, the Committee therefore entrenched the idea of small firms as a 'sector' and as a distinctive political constituency to be addressed by government (Binks and Coyne, 1983).

Advisory Services

Beyond the proposed Division, the recommendations were generally directed against greater intervention by the government in matters specifically affecting small firms. An example of this stance is provided by the Committee's position on advisory services provided to small firms. The initial internal paper on advisory services prepared by the Secretariat (BT360/9/79, TNA) suggested that it was not clear that small firms want advisory services (even if free). The rationale for the provision of advice related to the lack of financial and management expertise (including 'modern management techniques', p.4). However, it was highlighted that there was already a lot of government activity and wider provision of this type of support (the paper notes that the National Economic Development Council [NEDC] listed 247 bodies already providing services), albeit perhaps poorly coordinated and that the government had asked the Jarratt Working Party to rationalise this provision.

The paper discussed consultancy grants after a recent pilot was conducted in Bristol and Glasgow that offered to cover 50% of consultancy costs for firms with less than 500 employees. There were some concerns raised about the value of the scheme, including how it was engaged with by consultants. Overall, the paper argued against subsidising: 'We have to answer the question why those businesses which cannot meet the time cost of efficient operation (which includes the cost of necessary services) should not be allowed to go to the wall' (p.3). It did discuss a range of alternatives including 'a computer-linked information service like those in America and Japan' (p.6), although this did not feature in the Committee's final recommendations on advisory services.

In the final report, the Committee set out the conditions to be met before any advisory service should be provided, or subsidised, by government. It established a high, if somewhat flexible, bar (Bolton, 1971, p.346). The conditions set out by the Committee were subdivided between those required to justify *any* service provision by government: that the service was needed and that it was not, or could not, be provided by private enterprise. Two additional conditions were set out to justify *free or subsidised* provision, namely that there would be economic benefits to the nation that outweighed its costs and that those making use of such services could not be expected to pay for the full cost of the services (ibid.). While allowing for export services, which were not exclusive to small firms, and possible cases on social grounds for the support of rural and craft industries, the Committee found no examples of existing management advisory services meeting their conditions for subsidy (ibid., p.347).

The Committee did recognise, however, a justifiable case for establishing a network of Small Firms Advisory Bureaux (ibid.) that would serve as a signposting and referral service for small firms. This recommendation was broadly in agreement with recent Conservative proposals for 'Small Business Centres' (see Chapter 6). It also reflected a view expressed in submissions highlighting degrees of overlap and duplication of functions. Signposting and referral therefore seemed the most appropriate course of action. Reporting to the Small Firms Division, the Bureaux would serve a dual purpose of guiding small firms in relation to government policy, among other things, as well as providing a communications channel from the small firms to the government (ibid., p.141). For instance, it was hoped that the Bureaux would help address the 'information gap' (ibid., p.348) identified by the Committee in respect of small firms' knowledge about available sources of finance.

Access to Finance

The Committee's final report argued against a need for positive discrimination from government towards small firms with regard to finance. Small firms' difficulties in accessing finance were acknowledged. However, they were explained in terms of lending to small firms being more costly than to large firms, central government constraints placed on institutions and a 'lamentable ignorance of the sources available to meet specific financial needs' among small firm owners and their advisers (ibid.).

Nevertheless, the Committee did allow that should some future decision be taken to subsidise finance to small firms, this should be organised through the existing system rather than creating an official body providing finance directly (ibid., p.192). In this way, amidst the nuance and the disagreements, while the Bolton Report did not recommend action, it did highlight the 'Macmillan gap' in small firm access to finance as a topic for ongoing future debate and consideration for policy interventions (e.g. see The Financing of Small Firms, Interim Report of the Committee to Review the Functioning of the Financial Institutions, 1979, Cmnd. 7503).

The Government Response

In early Autumn 1971, the Committee's report was circulated within government and the civil service to consider the government's response when the Committee's work was presented to Parliament. The Prime Minister was said to consider it important, when the report was published, to be able to announce policy decisions on as many of the Committee's recommendations as possible (T342/116, TNA). In late September 1971, a letter from Downing Street to the DTI indicated that the Prime Minister had requested a task force be established to undertake this task of reaching policy decisions (FV62/45/2, TNA).

Interdepartmental meetings were held in October 1971 to discuss how the government would respond to the Committee's recommendations. Nevertheless, reflecting the dynamic context in which the Committee was operating (see Chapter 6), certain of its recommendations were already overtaken by events. Treasury files concerning the Committee's recommendations noted that since the report was prepared, the government had taken action to improve the position of small firms with regard to finance supply, for instance lifting restrictions on hire purchase (T342/116a, TNA). Records from an interdepartmental meeting indicate, furthermore, that the Chancellor had implemented some of the Committee's recommendations in the previous Budget (T342/116b, TNA). Internal discussions noted that the essence of the report was contained less in the specific recommendations and more in the underlying theme that government should develop a policy towards small firms (FV62/45, TNA).

In a submission from civil servants in the DTI to the Secretary of State, the recommendations on the machinery of government were presented in detail, including for a new Small Firms Division (T342/116c, TNA). The Secretary of State was informed that the arguments in favour of such a proposal were political, whereas those arguments against the proposed change were largely practical. The case *for* the creation of a Small Firms Division in the DTI centred on it providing evidence that the government was listening to the complaints of small firm owners and committed to helping small businesses. The practical case *against* adopting the recommendation appeared to centre on the Minister having only limited power. The Small Firms Minister would not, for instance, be formulating fiscal or taxation policy. Moreover, the creation of a small firms 'client group' would cut across recent changes by the government to reorganise lines of responsibility by function.

The proposal to create a Small Firms Division seems, in fact, to have been more contentious than this among other parts of the civil service and government. There were questions raised about whether it really was the case that small firms constituted a 'sector' and what proportion of these firms actually provided the beneficial functions for the economy highlighted in the Bolton Report (FV62/45/57, TNA). Writing with Bannock in 1989, Alan Peacock recalled this time from the perspective of a former civil servant (and, in 1973–1976, Chief Economic Adviser to the DTI):

> I remember very well when the Bolton Committee on Small Firms first appeared and how sceptically it was regarded by powerful politicians and civil servants who had all too readily accepted the Galbraithian thesis that the small person in business was a tedious anachronism.
>
> (Bannock and Peacock, 1989, p.3)

The proposed Small Firms Division was also controversial in relation to Ministers' stated strategy of reducing the size and functions of the central government. Heath's Conservative government had come to power intent on radical changes to reduce the size and role of government in the industry (Blackaby, 1978) and had published its intent the previous autumn (Cmnd. 4515 and Cmnd. 4506). In particular, the Central Policy Review Staff created by Heath to advise on strategy and policy (James, 1986) appears to have been against creating a small firms lobby in government, with records indicating the view that 'there was and should be no such animal as "small firms policy"' (T342/116, Qg/0226, TNA).

Nonetheless, writing to the Treasury, Sir Antony Part of the DTI advised that his Secretary of State would press for the Small Firms Division and a Minister with special responsibility for small firms (T342/116, TNA). This Division would then be in place to further consider the specific recommendations arising from the Committee. The position of the DTI in favour of the Small Firms Division was also reinforced in a minute sent from John Davies to the Prime Minister, with a copy of his draft speech to the House of Commons when announcing publication of the Committee's Report. In the minute, Davies highlights the emphasis placed on the problems facing small businesses during the 1970 General Election campaign and the pledge to consider the Committee's recommendations (T342/116d, TNA).

The Report of the Committee of Inquiry on Small Firms was announced in the House of Commons by Secretary of State for Trade and Industry John Davies on 3 November 1971. The Minister welcomed the Report as the first study of its kind, noting that 'it will stand as a landmark for many years to come'. He also indicated his acceptance of the report's major recommendations:

> First, in order that the place of small firms in the economy should be continuously watched and their interests be taken into account in the formulation of policies, the Committee recommends that in my Department a Minister should be designated as responsible for small firms and that a small firms division should be set up. I accept both these recommendations. I propose to give the ministerial responsibility to my hon. Friend the Under-Secretary of State for Industry, and a division will be set up whose primary function will be to support him in this work.
>
> (HC Deb, 3 November 1971, 825 c188.)

Davies went on to explain how the government would proceed with further consideration of the Committee's recommendations or through bringing proposals to the House. Although the government would not be accepting all of the Committee's recommendations, for instance doubling the limit on industrial development certificates, this was to be kept under review.

The Immediate Response to the Bolton Report

Already in the weeks leading up to the publication of the Committee's final report, the work of the Committee gained Press coverage through the release of its research studies. *The Times* reported on the issue of *The Small Unit in the Distributive Trades* and *The Role of Small Firms in Innovation in the United Kingdom since 1945*. Later that month, the same newspaper highlighted the publication of *The Dynamics of Small Firms* (T342/116e, TNA). Although none of the research reports were discussed in any great detail, it is interesting to note that the release of research reports feeding into the Committee was given any coverage in the National Press ahead of the main report's presentation to Parliament.

Responses to the published report and its recommendations unfolded over the late Autumn of 1971 and into early 1972. Organisations representing small business owners responded with a mix of disappointment and cautious welcome. The Smaller Businesses Association (SBA) was quoted as expressing disappointment at the 'complacency' shown towards small firms in the report. While satisfied that the Committee had recognised the important role played by small firms in the economy, the SBA considered that the Committee had been 'over optimistic' of the prospects facing these firms. The Association of British Chambers of Commerce welcomed the proposed role for a small firms Minister but expressed scepticism on the need for local advisory Bureaux, given the potential for overlap with the efforts and existing work of local Chambers of Commerce (T342/116f, TNA).

The Confederation of British Industry (CBI), which was co-sponsoring a conference on the future of small firms (T342/116g, TNA), was generally positive towards the Committee's recommendations. In a memo to the NEDC (T340/120/NEDC(72)3, TNA), the CBI highlighted its role in the Committee's creation and expressed satisfaction that certain of the CBI's own recommendations had been incorporated. It was also keen for progress to be made on enacting the Committee's recommendations. News reports of a speech delivered by CBI Director-General Campbell Adamson carried calls for the government to implement more of the Committee's recommendations and indicated that the CBI would be establishing two working parties to consider the report.

Reactions among commentators in the Press more widely seem to have been somewhat negative. Business and politics periodical, *The Economist* described the report as 'a disappointment' noting that:

> The only criticism of successive governments was that of unintentional neglect.

> (*The Economist*, T342/116h, TNA)

The dismissive tone of the article noted that many of the recommendations would occur through legislation already anticipated from the government. Furthermore, the article criticised the recommended government support for the proposed Small Firms Advisory Bureaux, arguing that users of such services ought to pay for them.

Writing in *The Sunday Times*, Philip Clarke and Nicholas Faith commented that the Bolton Report 'may well stand as a historical monument – a study which analysed in great detail a situation that had started to change even before the ink on its 436 pages was dry' (7 November 1971, T342/116i, TNA). Some of these changes were contained in the

Budget of 1971 while other changes were attributed to a more sympathetic attitude among the credit institutions. Clarke and Faith suggested that, although the small businessman (sic) had been portrayed clearly, recommendations such as for Small Firm Advisory Bureaux were out of step with the busy day-to-day realities of running a small business, and the general disposition of those doing so. Nevertheless, the authors considered that the report was overdue and criticised the failures of both Labour and Conservative post-war governments for their neglect of the small firm.

Despite the rather mixed response to the report, it clearly established a category of firms based on size (less than 200 employees) within the machinery of government and within wider political discourse. At once recognising and, through practical necessity, smoothing over the heterogeneity of such a category, the report allowed attention to be focused on the challenges considered to hinder this 'sector'. Moreover, as we discuss in the final chapter, despite the equivocations of the Bolton Committee, the potential challenges facing small firms that it discussed, such as those associated with obtaining finance and coping with burdensome government requirements, have continued to feature in discussions of small firms and enterprise policymaking in the 50 years since the publication of its report.

Conclusion

The Bolton Committee was tasked with analysing a major part of the national economy and formulating recommendations for government at a time when small firms were generally not well represented in government circles and robust information about them was in short supply. Despite these significant hurdles, the Committee amassed research and information and developed a long list of recommendations. Principal among these recommendations was that the machinery of government should understand more about small firms and consider their interests more explicitly. Coming down against positive discrimination by government towards small firms, the Committee's recommendation for a Small Firms Division and associated DTI Minister was somewhat controversial given the broader direction of the Heath government. Yet, making an explicit show of support for small firms was consistent with how the Conservatives had positioned themselves, especially in contrast to the previous Labour government.

Beyond Westminster, the report seems to have been altogether less controversial. As might have been anticipated, groups seeking to represent small firms wished that the Committee had gone further in some respects but still found some positives in the work. In the Press, some commentators appeared underwhelmed by the recommendations produced as a result of the Committee's efforts, partly as government actions had already started to address certain complaints. Ultimately, the very existence of the Bolton Committee and its prompting to create a function in government focused on the interests of small firms mark a significant shift in the relationship between government and small firms. In the final chapter, we consider the extent of this shift as we consider the longer-term impact of the Bolton Committee.

References

Bannock, G. (1971). *The Juggernauts: The age of the big corporation* (1st edition). London: Weidenfeld and Nicolson.

Bannock, G. and Peacock, A. (1989). *Governments and small business* (introduction by Alan Peacock). London: Paul Chapman Publishing.

Binks, M. and Coyne, J. (1983). *The Birth of Enterprise: An Analytical and Empirical Study of the Growth of Small Firms*. London: The Institute of Economic Affairs.

Blackaby, F.T. (1978). Narrative. In: F.T. Blackaby (ed.) *British economic policy, 1960–74*. Cambridge: Cambridge University Press, pp.11–76.

Bolton, J.E. (1971). *Committee of inquiry on small firms*, Cmnd. 4811. London: H.M.S.O. (reprint).

BT262/20/CSF77, TNA: 16th Committee meeting, 4 December 1969.

BT262/20/CSF142, TNA: 25th Committee meeting, 26 March 1970.

BT262/20/CSF201, TNA: 40th Committee meeting, 15 July 1970.

BT262/21/265, TNA: 51st Committee meeting, 2 November 1970.

BT262/21/320, TNA: 62nd Committee meeting, 18 January 1971.

BT262/21/CSF333, TNA: 66th Committee meeting, 17 February 1971.

BT262/21/CSF336, TNA: 67th Committee meeting, 24 February 1971.

BT262/21/CSF347, TNA: 71st Committee meeting, 24 March 1971.

BT262/21/CSF365, TNA: 81st Committee meeting, 12 May 1971.

BT360/10/124, TNA: Sources of Finance, discussion paper prepared by Secretariat.

BT360/9/79, TNA: Advisory Services and Consultancy Grants.

Cmnd. 4506. (1970). *The reorganisation of central government*, Presented to Parliament by the Prime Minister and Minister for the Civil Service.

Cmnd. 4515. (1970). *New policies for public spending*, Presented to Parliament by the Chancellor of the Exchequer.

Craig, F.W.S. (1990). *British General Election manifestos 1959–1987* (3rd edition). Aldershot: Parliamentary Research Services, Dartmouth (publisher). (*A Better Tomorrow,* Conservative Party, 1970).

FV62/45, TNA: Note, 6 October 1971.

FV62/45/2, TNA: Letter from 10 Downing Street, 27 September 1971.

FV62/45/57, TNA: Interdepartmental meeting held at the DTI on 4 October 1971 to consider the implementation of the Bolton Committee recommendations.

HC Deb (1971) vol.825 col.188, John Davies, MP, 3 November.

James, S. (1986). The Central Policy Review Staff, 1970–1983. *Political Studies*, XXXIV: 423–440.

Radcliffe, C. (1959). *Committee on the working of the monetary system, Report*, Cmnd. 827. London: H.M.S.O.

Research Unit (1972). *A postal questionnaire survey of small firms: Non-financial data, tables, definitions and notes*. London: H.M.S.O.

T340/120/NEDC(72)3, TNA: The Bolton Committee of Inquiry on Small Firms, Memorandum by the Confederation of British Industry.

T342/116, Qg/0226, TNA: Cabinet Office memorandum to the Department of Trade and Industry, 22 October 1971.

T342/116, TNA: Letter from Department of Trade and Industry to Treasury Chambers, 27 October 1971.

T342/116a, TNA: Memo, Bolton Committee of Enquiry on Small Firms, 29 October 1971.

T342/116b, TNA: Interdepartmental meeting held at the DTI on 4 October 1971 to consider the implementation of the Bolton Committee recommendations.

T342/116c, TNA: Report of Bolton Committee of Inquiry on Small Firms, Submissions to the Secretary of State DTI on the recommendations on machinery of government, 22 October 1971.

T342/116d, TNA: Letter to the Prime Minister from John Davies, 2 November 1971.

T342/116e, TNA: *The Times*, 'Training period for aspiring small traders among Bolton report recommendations', Malcolm Brown, 18 October 1971. Press coverage of research reports: *The small unit in the distributive trades* and *The role of small firms in innovation in the United Kingdom since 1945*.

T342/116f, TNA: *Financial Times*, 'Bolton Committee Report: New DTI Division and Minister should sponsor small firms', Harold Bolter, 4 November 1971.

T342/116g, TNA: *Financial Times*, 'Conference to discuss future of small firms', 10 November 1971.

The Economist, T342/116h, TNA: 'No case for aid', 6 November 1971.

The Financing of Small Firms, Interim Report of the Committee to Review the Functioning of the Financial Institutions (1979), Cmnd. 7503.

The Sunday Times (1971). 'Enter, cautiously, Mr Nicholas Ridley the new protector of the small business', Philip Clarke and Nicholas Faith, 7 November (also T342/116i, TNA).

Thomson, A. (2016). *Small business, education and management: The life and times of John Bolton*. Abingdon: Routledge.

8 Bolton 50 Years On

Introduction

This book has presented an analysis of how the 'path-breaking' Committee of Inquiry on Small Firms was formed, how it worked and how it produced its report and recommendations. Our analysis has highlighted the difficulties encountered by the Committee in getting to grips with a hitherto overlooked yet hugely significant class of businesses. Analysis of departmental records, Committee minutes, submissions of evidence and commissioned research reports shows how the arrival of small business and entrepreneurship on the UK's national policy agenda was integral to debates around government's relationship with industry.

The Committee was established and progressed with the key influence coming from the principal employer representative body, the Confederation of British Industry, and with relatively limited involvement from the Trades Union Congress. This might help to explain the lack of attention paid to the employees of small businesses, and the propagation of a 'small is beautiful' perspective on working life (Rainnie, 1989). Further, with particular relevance for the Committee's recommendations, the Committee sat during a time when consensus on the role of government in matters of industry was being contested by an ideology of small government and free-market economics.

The heterogeneity of the small firms 'sector' of the economy also created challenges in identifying the voices of small firms, their concerns and potential remedies. A Small Firms Division, embedded in the previous political consensus but conflicting with the contemporary government ethos, offered one way to engage with these firms. However, it failed to resolve the inherent difficulties in engaging with such a large number of very different businesses. Nonetheless, while the recommendations offered by the Committee fell short of advocating significant positive

DOI: 10.4324/9781003119142-8

discrimination for small firms, the report entrenched small firms as a distinctive category and elaborated specific problems facing these businesses, such as access to finance.

To understand the influence of the Bolton Report, it is important to recognise the ambiguities embedded within it as a result of the turbulent political context in which it was produced. The Committee was established under a Labour government and developed through the auspices of industrial coordination and the National Economic Development Council. However, after several delays, the Committee came to produce its report under what appeared to be the radically new, small government agenda of Heath's Conservative administration in 1970. While embedded within the Committee's work was an analysis of the problems facing small firms, an assumption of government action and a voice for small business as a new 'sector', the Committee's recommendations acquired a tone and appearance more attuned with the new government's preferences. This meant the report could be used to serve differing political ends and this became important for its later influence during further changes in political focus and is central to understanding its 'path-breaking' nature.

Bolton, in Reflection

The Bolton Report's Preface expresses the hope that, while primarily addressed to government, the report would also be of use and interest to trade associations, small business owners and to scholars. However, as Bannock noted in 1976, 'perhaps not unnaturally the report did not seize the imagination of the public and interest was not sustained' (p.6). Indeed, given the general neglect of small firms in the years prior to the Committee, it might have been somewhat surprising had the report achieved the wider appeal aspired to by the Committee. Attitudes towards entrepreneurship and small business would come to change, but this was not a change that took place in the 1970s or directly in response to arguments made in the Committee's report. Excluding the creation of a Small Firms Division and ongoing changes to areas such as taxation, there was no major change in attitude towards small firms and many owner-managers continued to feel ignored or mistreated by government.

John Bolton himself seems to have regarded political responses with a degree of disappointment. By the mid-1970s, Bolton was being quoted as saying that the changes made to address the problems facing small firms were being replaced by new burdens. On the matter of excessive government paperwork through statistics gathering, initially changes eased the burden on small firms but these were viewed as having been undone by new requirements such as those around value-added tax (VAT). Bolton also expressed concern that additional legislation, however desirable the aims might be, continued to disproportionately burden the small business owner. Drawing a contrast with the nations of Japan and the United States, where Bolton saw encouragement for entrepreneurs, in the UK '... government, unions, academics, the media – indeed, the Establishment as a whole – seem not to care at all about the font of free enterprise, the small businessman' (see Snobel, 1976, p.17).

As Thomson's biography details, Bolton continued publicly speaking out on a small firms agenda throughout the 1970s and into the mid-1980s. From Thomson's account, it appears that Bolton recognised how small firms were rising up the political agenda, but he retained his frustration that there was much more to be done. In his Foreword to a collection of academic research papers (*Bolton 20 Years On*), Bolton (1991) considered that:

> Despite the government's best efforts to improve things, it seems to me that it still needs to do more to reduce unnecessary burdens on business, which would do so much to contribute to economic welfare and that would enhance rather than deplete tax revenues.
>
> (p.x)

Notably, Thomson narrates Bolton's regret that, during the Committee, he had pursued the practical politics of Whitehall rather than propose more radical interventions. Such an approach had, in his view, eased the adoption of the Committee's recommendations, but that, in retrospect, positive discrimination in favour of small firms might have been appropriate (see Thomson, 2016, p.155). Bannock's subsequent account of the Committee also alludes to this tension, noting how it had '... agonized at some length on the issue of whether positive discrimination in favour of small firms could be justified'. He explains how without clear evidence that the small firms sector was declining so far that it could no longer fulfil a seedbed function in the economy, the Committee felt positive discrimination could not be justified (1989, p.17).

The Committee found that governments had not been deliberately seeking to damage small firms but rather that they had insufficient regard for their interests and the impacts of policies upon them. In response, the creation of a Small Firms Division was seen as a means to remedy this situation although, perhaps for Bolton himself, it was unclear how much had really altered.

Political U-Turns and Implementing Bolton

Heath's period in office (1970–1974) saw his government accused of at least four significant U-turns (Seldon, 2014). First, there was not a radical programme of privatisation. It was soon apparent that, faced with pressures such as unemployment, the government was starting to revise its commitment to disengagement, for instance, through the rescue of shipyards on the Upper Clyde in 1972 (Blackaby, 1978). Second, regional policy was reintroduced (e.g. Regional Development Grants for industry in assisted regional areas) and Wilks (1999) argues that, contrary to the small government pitch of the 1970 election, sections of the subsequent 1972 Industry Act 'contained some of the most interventionist powers to direct and subsidize industry ever taken outside wartime'. Third, there was a return to tripartite negotiation and engagement with trade unions. Finally, there was a significant increase in public expenditure. For Wilks (1999, p.182), these U-turns represented a 'rejection of the liberal individualism expressed in the early days of the Heath Government which has, rightly, been seen as the precursor to the Thatcherite revolution of the 1980s'.

King (1979) explains that the right of the Tory party was unhappy, for example, with the shift towards more tripartite and accommo-dating attitudes towards trade unions. In opposition prior to 1970, it had perhaps been easier to call for free markets, smaller government and for entrepreneurs to be framed as the seedbed of future prosperity. Further, pre-election, the Conservatives needed small business owners' votes, so doing things that showed support for them made electoral sense. Nonetheless, despite the apparent contradiction with the agenda proposed when they were elected, some, such as Christopher Chataway, who was appointed Minister for Industrial Development in April 1972, sought to argue that a more engaged approach between government and industry was wholly consistent with Conservative values. In the 1972 CPC pamphlet 'New Deal for Industry: Government and Industry on the Threshold of Europe', Chataway argued that government inter-vention was necessary, in light of international competition. This was particularly important because '... the governments of our industrial rivals regard themselves as the allies of their industry, that in a favourite phrase the British government has continued to play cricket while others are involved in a much rougher game' (p.10).

More than had previously been the case in the UK, small firms were now recognised by government as having a significant role to play in benefiting the economy and tackling the challenges the country faced (Leyshon, 1982). Chataway highlighted the progress of the UK government in respect of small firms. He pointed to the implementation of most of the Bolton Committee's recommendations and to the recent announcement regarding the establishment of a national small firms advisory service. By Bannock's (1976) reckoning, of the 58 recommendations made by the Committee, of which 56 required government action, and just six were rejected outright.

Of those six recommendations rejected outright, three were related to the impacts of taxation on small firms. In detailing those rejected recommendations on tax, however, Bannock points to where legislation had subsequently gone some way to addressing the concerns raised, for instance, in reforms to shortfall assessments. Two recommendations in favour of easing restrictive practices legislation for small firms were also rejected, citing potential concerns over harming consumer interests. Finally, the Committee's recommendation to create a single, comprehensive databank of business records was rejected citing concerns over confidentiality.

In 1973, the Small Firms Division's role was extended to include further research. This included an aim 'to form a view of the present and future role of small firms in all industries in which they are important' (Hansard, HC Deb. 8 March 1973 vol.852 cols.204-5) and important factors such as competition policy, government procurement and the potential impact of joining the European Economic Community. Nonetheless, in Bannock's view the Small Firms Division undertook to fulfil the letter, if not the full spirit, of the role imagined for it by the Committee, despite limited resources. Bannock (1976) suggests that the resource or organisational constraints did not represent a significant limit on the Division's effectiveness, more important was a failure in government and beyond to appreciate the particular problems facing small firms. In an interesting echo of the report (paragraph 9.4), Bannock ties this ignorance to an unwillingness or inability of small firm owners, and their employees, to form effective political lobbies to inform government and wider society of their concerns.

The government action taken in response to the Bolton Report's recommendations was further debated in the House of Lords in 1973. Niall Macpherson, Lord Drumalbyn and previously a Joint-Minister of State for Trade, spoke as a Minister without portfolio on behalf of the government. He explained that 'The Government wholeheartedly accepted the Report and immediately went ahead with the task of evaluating and, where possible, implementing the recommendations contained in it'. Macpherson went on to explain those recommendations that had been implemented before the Committee reported (e.g. on tax) and emphasised the creation of the Small Firms Division. This was

followed by the creation of a signposting service to support small firms
in the form of Small Firm Information Centres, with offices opening 'in
London, Glasgow, Cardiff and Birmingham, and in six other centres in
the Provinces'.

Macpherson highlighted the Committee's stance against subsidies
and that:

> Government should only provide a service if it is needed and pri-
> vate enterprise cannot or will not provide it, and should only sub-
> sidise services if the economic benefit to the nation deriving from
> them is greater than their cost, and the users cannot pay or should
> not be expected to pay their full cost.

He also explained the difficulties facing the Small Firms Division and
the relevant Minister given that many of the recommendations related
to other government departments. Perhaps as a result, while some
recommendations had been implemented in full, others were 'in part'
and this may have been supported by the appointment of 13 liaisons
from other departments. Some policies were seen to benefit small firms
(e.g. tax relief on loans), others specifically targeted them (e.g. reduced
corporation tax for firms with profits less than £25,000). Firms no
longer had to disclose their turnover if it was not above £250,000, the
processes for issuing requests for data from firms were under scrutiny,
industrial development certificates were abolished in designated development areas and exemptions were being discussed for training levies.

While such actions did not bring about radical change in the position of small firms, they continued to position small firms as a specific
'sector' or constituency. This is clear in Macpherson's conclusion:

> Small firms now have a voice to speak for them within Government,
> and it is a voice which is speaking; it is a Division in the D.T.I.; it
> is an officer in each of 13 other Departments to watch over their
> needs, and a network of offices all over the country to help them to
> look after themselves and to make their proper contribution to the
> economic and social life of the nation.
>
> (HC Deb. 8 March 1973 vol.852 cols.204-5)

Nonetheless, tensions remained between government and the emerging voice of small business. Despite their general tendency towards
the Conservative Party, some small business owners viewed the party's
small business credentials with scepticism as it appeared more inclined
towards large business interests. An interesting point made by King

(1979, pp.161–162) is that perhaps in some cases the idea of a 'small business' in the minds of the Conservative Party was different from that of small traders. For Conservatives, a 'small business' could be a small employer, which is actually a relatively large organisation when compared with the self-employed trader or worker – so tax cuts to help the 'small business' might satisfy the small employer who is doing well but not be relevant for the self-employed tradesperson.

Labour Return to Power

Returning to government in 1974, Labour rushed through a legislative agenda (anticipating another vote). While not specifically anti-small business, this agenda did small firms few favours. These efforts were reflected in the October 1974 manifesto which devoted more space and attention to the small business. The subsequent period of government under Labour (1974–1979) saw limited engagement with small firms and repeated conflict within the small firms lobby over issues such as the VAT and the introduction of an 8% Type 4 National Insurance on the taxable profits of the self-employed.

However, King (1979) argues that the Labour government was not as anti-small business as sometimes portrayed and that it allowed concessions in its 1974–1975 legislative programme. The Bolton Report still proved relevant in terms of how small firms were defined by government. For example, in 1976, responding to a question about how small firms were defined by his department, Labour Minister of State at the Department of Industry Alan Williams responded that 'The Department adopted the statistical definition of small firms originated by the Bolton Committee', with variation in definition for different industries (HC Deb. 28 July 1976 vol.916 col.275). The definition would later often be simplified for specific policy eligibility criteria (e.g. a scheme eligible for firms with less than 25 employees without targeting specific sectors, see, e.g. Mallett and Wapshott, 2020) but the Bolton Committee's report remained a persistent touchstone in UK enterprise policy definitions of small firms.

While Heath's Conservatives had retreated from monetarism to the embedded assumptions of Keynesianism in the face of rising unemployment, by the mid-1970s, there was increasingly widespread concern that Keynesian approaches were not suitable for the crises the country faced. Labour Chancellor Denis Healey considered letting unemployment increase in order to fight skyrocketing inflation, representing an early move towards the types of policy that would come to reshape UK economic policymaking. For Hall (1992), the Labour government's move towards monetarism was less a refutation of Keynesianism and more a signal of the increasing influence of financial interests through financial markets (and as a result of an indebted economy and changing gilt market) and the diminishing of trade union influence from 1976 onwards.

Nonetheless, enterprise policy initiatives did remain, and the European Economic Community also provided additional funding for regional policy activity, including support for small firms. In 1977, Bob Cryer, Secretary of State for Industry, set out the general provision that had been established as a result of the post-Bolton activity:

> Small firms in England are eligible for a wide range of Government assistance, which is generally available throughout the United Kingdom to encourage the growth and expansion of firms of every size. In particular, most of the sectoral schemes in operation under Section 8 of the Industry Act 1972 contain special provisions for assistance towards the cost of consultancy studies for small firms; in two schemes, the minimum size for investment projects has been reduced; and 108 individual terrace or nursery units for occupation by small firms are being built. Small firms can also call on the services of the small firms information centres at any stage of their development.
>
> (HC Deb. vol.928 col.496 22 March 1977)

Beesley and Hamilton (1984, p.228) characterised the response of governments during the 1970s to the Bolton Committee's recommendations as being 'the ad hoc development of a small firms policy'. Nonetheless, the clear identification of a 'small firms' constituency and an official statistical definition created a consistent thread that drew together ad hoc policy measures that had traditionally been disconnected (Leyshon, 1982). It is this way that the Bolton Committee and its report can be considered to have established UK enterprise policy.

Thatcher and the Enterprise Culture

Late in 1978, the Labour government was damaged by a series of high-profile industrial disputes, 'suddenly bringing Britain to the point of chaos' (Rubinstein, 2003, p.315). A vote of confidence lost by the Labour government (by one vote) led to a General Election and, ultimately, a new Conservative government led by Margaret Thatcher. The Conservative election campaign had focused on economic discipline, anti-union measures and 'denationalization'. This time, however, the party was determined to fully pursue their plans (Thatcher famously declaring that 'To those waiting with bated breath for that favourite media catchphrase, the "U" turn, I have only one thing to say. "You turn if you want to. The lady's not for turning"' (Thatcher, 1980).

Hall (1992) highlights how, whereas Heath had faced a deeply entrenched belief in Keynesianism, Thatcher pursued the monetarist alternative at a time when these ideas had already been implemented by the previous Labour government were more clearly elaborated and articulated and had received institutional support from economists, the City and the media. Nonetheless, the new agenda was not entirely focused on 'small government'. As Hall (1986, pp.290–291) makes clear, while a key focus of the Thatcher government was the reinforcing of market mechanisms due to a belief that this would rejuvenate the economy, this 'required a great deal of state intervention in order to alter many longstanding practices and institutions'.

Bechhofer and Elliott (1981, p.192) saw an ideological appeal to 'a simpler, freer, more competitive economy ... in which the invisible hand steers individual competition along paths of efficiency, prosperity and freedom'. The Bolton Report reinforced this focus by entrenching small business and entrepreneurship as a legitimate focus of government attention. Smaller businesses had also become more prominent as a result of significant economic restructuring (Mallett and Wapshott, 2017). As large firms decreased the size of their operations, they created more opportunities for small businesses as they fragmented their operations through decentralisation (e.g. more small plants), devolvement (e.g. franchising) and disintegration (e.g. subcontracting). Small firms were now embraced as representing a form of individualism, freedom and personal responsibility in the new era of free markets and small government.

Thatcher was very explicit in relating her political agenda to this ideology through the creation of an 'enterprise culture'. This sought to encourage a particular set of social values based on self-reliance and self-help (and in opposition to a 'dependency culture', e.g. through the Enterprise Allowance Scheme, see Burrows, 1991; Mallett and Wapshott, 2020). This set of values was seen as embodied in the independent entrepreneur and the government set out to influence public attitudes towards small business and entrepreneurship. The enterprise culture often lacked clarity or a rigorous elaboration in policy terms, but it nonetheless provided a way to make sense of the changes many people were experiencing, for example, as they moved into self-employment (perhaps now as a subcontractor rather than employee) or as a member of a small firm (perhaps rather than as part of a unionised workforce in a large company or nationalised industry).

In addition to the Enterprise Allowance Scheme for those who were unemployed, a wide range of other schemes and initiatives were launched, including a Small Firms Loan Guarantee Scheme, a Business Start-Up Scheme (to provide tax relief for private investors), a Business Expansion Scheme, Business and Technical Advisory Services and many others. Many of these ideas existed before the Bolton Committee. This is not to say that Bolton exercised no influence. For example, a 1984 memo raising ongoing issues regarding form filling focused on recommendations from Bolton (including a copy of the relevant section) (FV96/64, TNA). However, much of the work in developing enterprise policy at this time involved gathering new data and new ideas. For example, a new review into support for small firms was initiated by the British Overseas Trade Board in 1983 that focused on export-related activities and concerns about small firms' ability to access finance to support such activities (FV96/65, TNA).

It was primarily the scale of government intervention in relation to small firms that was unparalleled by any previous UK government and this continued apace. For example, after Thatcher had left power but the Conservatives remained in government, Business Link was formed. This was a UK-wide, franchise-based business support service shaped by central government. By 1996, government spending on Business Link had reached £130 million per year (HC Deb. 6 November 1996 vol.284 col.1222) and was seen by some commentators as essentially a nationalisation of business support services (Priest, 1999). Clearly, there were tensions between a small government agenda and the interventions required to support small businesses.

There is no doubting the significance of the changes brought about through Thatcher and the enterprise culture in the UK. These were changes that persisted and that established a scale for UK enterprise policy that continues today (Mallett and Wapshott, 2020). However, the extent to which these ideas were successfully 'exported' internationally has been questioned. Detailing an account of the enterprise culture in Hungary, Ray (1991) recognises how aspects of Thatcherism had been adopted, including some of the language, but that such changes were being implemented in a very different context from that in which they had emerged.

Highlighting the importance of national context serves as a reminder that, at the time of the Bolton Committee, the UK was lagging behind other nations in terms of research and policy towards small firms and entrepreneurship. We have noted elsewhere in this book how the

Committee members looked overseas to learn what the governments of other nations were doing in respect of small firms, but beyond differences in bureaucratic structures, deeper-rooted differences should also be acknowledged. Gibb (1982, p.182), for instance, identifies 'a deeper (and longer standing) philosophical base in West Germany than in the UK' for small firms policy. In addition to politics, it is therefore also useful to consider the wider impacts of the Bolton Committee and its work.

The Impact of Bolton's Research

The work of the Bolton Committee stands not only as a political intervention but also as the largest UK study of, or relevant to, small firms of its time. Research into small firms of course predates the work of the Committee, for example Boswell's (1973) work was approved some six months before the Bolton Committee met. Other work, such as that of Woodward (1965/1980), had incorporated the study of small firms without being a project concerned solely with these businesses. Nevertheless, it remains the case that since the period of the Bolton Committee small firms have become a widely studied research focus.

During the years following the Committee's work, the influence of the report was deemed highly significant. Writing in the first issue of the *European Small Business Journal* (now *International Small Business Journal*), scholars James Curran and John Stanworth (1982, p.16) highlight the research reports commissioned by the Committee as providing a foundation for 'one of the most remarkable examples of sustained academic exploration of any area of business activity yet seen in Britain'. Writing some years later, introducing an edited collection of papers on small firms (20 years after Bolton), Stanworth and Gray (1991, p.xi) identified that the Bolton Report remained 'the single most important document of its kind ever published in Britain'.

The precise role of the Bolton Committee and its report in the increased focus of academic study on small firms is hard to pin down. The report is a staple reference in research on small firms, but the report itself is generally not discussed in detail. Reflecting on the period between the publication of the report and the late 1980s, Bannock (1989) notes how, in addition to the report, social and economic factors had influenced the rise of small firms on academic agendas. He also observed, however, that much of this work was being conducted in newer universities while among those of Oxford, Cambridge and the LSE small firms garnered little attention.

Today, of course, the knowledge produced by academics from a range of universities, including large-scale interventions such as those produced by the Enterprise Research Centre, not to mention the activities of the Institute for Small Business and Entrepreneurship, represent a research base the Bolton Committee members might only have dreamed of. It is interesting to recall David Storey's (1994, p.4) observation when introducing his landmark study of the small firms sector (cf. Young, 2012): returning to the Report, Storey reflects on how, 'whilst the economic environment has changed markedly, the agenda in those days was strikingly similar to that of today: financing, government intervention, the taxation system and macroeconomic policy'. We are struck by a similar consistency of focus and challenges as we write in 2021.

In other instances, the work and conclusions of the Committee itself have been subject to critique. Rainnie (1989) devotes a section of the appendix to his *Industrial Relations in Small Firms* monograph to engaging with the Bolton Report in some detail. Nevertheless, Rainnie's overwhelmingly critical assessment of the Committee's work and its 'reverential attitude to small business' (p.156) necessarily smooths over general attitudes towards small firms in government and the economy at the time, not to mention some of the stern criticisms reserved for small firms by the Committee. Perhaps, after ten years of Thatcher governments, the words of the Committee's report read differently than they did when they were written, embedded in a very different context for small firms.

More recently, Dannreuther and Perren (2013), in a wide-ranging examination of *The Political Economy of the Small Firm* have examined the role of the Bolton Committee in raising the profile of small firms politically and stimulating small firms policy. Within their reading of its work, Dannreuther and Perren (p.129) see that 'the Committee were able to grasp hegemonic power over the discursive construction of the small firm' at least for a while. As a discursive construction, the meaning associated with 'the small firm' was subject to political contest and became a vehicle for ideological projects such as the subsequent enterprise culture agenda.

However, there has been relatively little engagement with the Committee's postal survey, thought to be 'the best statistical analysis of the small firm sector ever attempted, and based on the largest sample ever used' (BT262/21/CSF372, TNA). There has been even less academic engagement with the research reports produced for the Committee. The Bolton Report has stood as a key moment when the 'small firm' became clearly embedded within the mechanisms of government, which led to an increased voice for these businesses and a joining together of otherwise ad hoc policy initiatives. In this way, the work of the Bolton Committee is hugely important. However, looking back now, it is difficult to see specific impacts directly arising from the substance of a great deal of the work conducted.

Conclusion

Notwithstanding its significant limitations, the creation of the Bolton Committee, its work and its final report served to acknowledge a new place for small firms and entrepreneurship on the national political agenda. The turbulent backdrop against which the Committee operated and the challenges inherent in its task contributed to recommendations that reflected uncertainties and contested positions of the era. Unresolved tensions over the role of government and its relationship to industry are apparent throughout the Committee's report and recommendations. Although small businesses had now re-emerged onto the political landscape, it was not until the subsequent developments of the enterprise culture under Thatcher that significant changes happened. The 'Thatcherite' agenda went a long way towards placing small business and entrepreneurship at the vanguard of social and economic policy reforms. This marked the establishment of a fresh consensus on how government relates to small firms; a consensus that belies the complex and uncertain beginnings of enterprise policy in the UK.

The political significance of the Bolton Report, as an artefact or a point of reference, still holds some power. This was apparent in the foreword to Lord Young's more recent contributions to the enterprise debate. Acting as an adviser to Prime Minister David Cameron, Young's 2012 report 'Make Business Your Business' opened by announcing 'This is the first comprehensive report on small and medium-sized enterprises (SMEs) since the Bolton Report of 1971, which was produced at a time when industry and commerce had hardly changed since the Victorian era.' It is noteworthy that, despite the increasing attention focused on small firms in the period since the Bolton Report, over 40 years later it remained the reference point as a comprehensive study of small firms by the UK government.

The development of the small firm 'sector' as a political constituency set out by the Bolton Committee created space for an enterprise policy agenda. It acted as a means of relating a range of somewhat ad hoc policies and initiatives together as what we would now refer to as an enterprise policy agenda. However, it provided little actionable detail about how it would be fulfilled. The Bolton Committee did lead to the creation of a Small Firms Division, but the subsequent developments through to Thatcher's enterprise culture and beyond were not inevitable. Political events and existing institutional arrangements would continue to exert influence and shape path dependencies; it was new ideas and coalitions of interests that then encouraged further development.

In the case of the Bolton Committee, it became apparent that acknowledging the importance of small firms and the difficulties they faced would not extend to recommending positive discrimination and would not entail working outside the established institutional framework for government–industry relations. The key contributions provided by the Bolton Committee did not produce radical change in government–industry relations in general terms. The overarching institutional arrangement remained stable. It was, however, path-breaking in how government related to small firms specifically. Establishing space for an enterprise policy agenda within the prevailing institutional framework (e.g. through the creation of the Small Firms Division) created opportunities for a small firms agenda to be promoted, but this did not determine how that agenda would go on to develop.

As the Conservative government (at our time of writing in 2021) sought enterprise policies as part of an agenda to tackle the economic and wider societal impacts of the COVID-19 pandemic, they are unlikely to have reached for a battered old copy of the 1971 Bolton Report. Nonetheless, the focus on small firms as a key constituency, the ways in which this has become embedded in UK political discourse and some of the mechanisms of government (including a Minister for Small Business, Consumers and Corporate Responsibility) do bear the legacy of the Bolton Committee's work. The tensions between free-market political parties focused on small government and the scale of government intervention to support small businesses also remain an important but often unspoken political challenge.

References

Bannock, G. (1976). *The smaller business in Britain and Germany*. London: Anglo-German Foundation/Wilton House Publications.

Bannock, G. (1989). Changing viewpoints. In: G. Bannock and A. Peacock (eds.) *Governments and small business*. London: Paul Chapman Publishing, pp.12–59.

Bechhofer, F. and Elliott, B. (1981). Petty property: The survival of a moral economy. In: F. Bechhofer and B. Elliott (eds.) *The petite bourgeoisie*. London: Palgrave Macmillan, pp.182–200.

Beesley, M.E. and Hamilton, R.T. (1984). Small firms' seedbed role and the concept of turbulence. *The Journal of Industrial Economics*, 33(2): 217–231.

110   *Bolton 50 Years On*

Blackaby, F.T. (1978). Narrative. In: F.T. Blackaby (ed.) *British economic policy, 1960–74.* Cambridge: Cambridge University Press, pp.11–76.

Bolton, J.E. (1991). Preface. In: J. Stanworth and C. Gray (eds.) *Bolton 20 years on: The small firm in the 1990s.* London: Small Business Research Trust/Paul Chapman Publishing, p.ix.

Boswell, J. (1973). *The rise and decline of small firms.* London: George Allen & Unwin.

BT262/21/CSF372, TNA: 84th Committee meeting, 2 June 1971.

Burrows, R. (1991). The discourse of the enterprise culture and the restructuring of Britain. In: J. Curran and R.A. Blackburn (eds.) *Paths of enterprise: The future of the small business.* London: Routledge, pp.17–33.

Chataway, C. (1972). *New Deal for industry: Government and industry on the threshold of Europe.* London: Conservative Political Centre, CPC No. 515.

Curran, J. and Stanworth, J. (1982). The small firm in Britain – Past, present and future. *European Small Business Journal,* 1(1): 16–25.

Dannreuther, C. and Perren, L. (2013). *The political economy of the small firm.* Abingdon: Routledge.

FV96/64, TNA: Memo in file 'Small firms: proposed removal of administrative and legislative burdens on employers' 11 May 1984.

FV96/65, TNA: Memo in file 'Small firms: review of assistance and services from the British Overseas Trade Board'.

Gibb, A. (1982). Small firms policy in Baden-Wurttenberg (sic): Some UK implications. In: D. Watkins, J. Stanworth and A. Westrip (eds.) *Stimulating small firms.* Aldershot: Gower.

Hall, P.A. (1986). The state and economic decline. In: B. Elbaum and W. Lazonick (eds.) *The decline of the British economy.* Oxford: Oxford University Press, pp.266–302.

Hall, P.A. (1992). The movement from Keynesianism to monetarism: Institutional analysis and British economic policy in the 1970s. In: S. Steinmo, K. Thelen and F. Longstreth (eds.) *Structuring politics: Historical institutionalism in comparative analysis.* Cambridge: Cambridge University Press, pp.90–113.

HC Deb (1973). vol.852 cols.204-5, Lord Macpherson, 8 March.

HC Deb (1976). vol.916 col.275, Alan Williams MP, 28 July.

HC Deb (1977). vol.928 col.496, Bob Cryer MP, 22 March.

HC Deb (1996). vol.284 col.1222, *Business Link,* 6 November.

King, R. (1979). The middle class revolt and the established parties. In: R. King and N. Nugent (eds.) *Respectable Rebels.* London: Hodder and Stoughton.

Leyshon, A. (1982). The UK government small business model – A review. *European Small Business Journal,* 1(1): 58–66.

Mallett, O. and Wapshott, R. (2017). Small business revivalism: Employment relations in small and medium-sized enterprises. *Work, Employment & Society,* 31(4): 721–728.

Mallett, O. and Wapshott, R. (2020). *A history of enterprise policy: Government, small business and entrepreneurship.* New York: Routledge.

Priest, S.J. (1999). Business Link services to small and medium-sized enterprises: Targeting, innovation, and charging. *Environment and Planning C: Government and Policy*, 17(2): 177–194.

Rainnie, A. (1989). *Industrial relations in small firms: Small isn't beautiful.* London: Routledge.

Ray, L. (1991). A Thatcher export phenomenon? The enterprise culture in Eastern Europe. In: R. Keat and N. Abercrombie (eds.) *Enterprise culture.* London: Routledge, pp.114–135.

Rubinstein, W.D. (2003). *Twentieth-century Britain: A political history.* Basingstoke: Palgrave Macmillan.

Seldon, A. (2014). The Heath government in history. In: S. Ball and A. Seldon (eds.) *The Heath government 1970–74: A reappraisal.* Abingdon: Routledge, pp.1–20.

Snobel, A. (1976). The plight of small firms. *Industrial Management*, 1 May 1976 URL: www.emerald.com/insight/content/doi/10.1108/eb056631/full/html Accessed 01.05.21.

Stanworth, J. and Gray, C. (1991). Acknowledgements. In J. Stanworth and C. Gray (eds.) *Bolton 20 years on: The small firm in the 1990s.* London: Small Business Research Trust/Paul Chapman Publishing, p.xi.

Storey, D.J. (1994). *Understanding the small business sector.* London: Routledge.

Thatcher, M. (1980). Leader's speech. URL: www.theguardian.com/politics/2007/apr/30/conservatives.uk1 Accessed 01.05.21.

Thomson, A. (2016). *Small business, education and management: The life and times of John Bolton.* Abingdon: Routledge.

Wilks, S. (1999). *In the public interest: Competition policy and the Monopolies and Mergers Commission.* Manchester: Manchester University Press.

Woodward, J. (1965/1980). *Industrial organization: Theory and practice* (2nd edition). Oxford: Oxford University Press.

Young, D. (2012) *Make business your business: A report on small business start-ups.* URN 12/827 Department for Business, Innovation and Skills. URL: https://assets.publishing.service.gov.uk/government/uploads/system/uploads/attachment_data/file/32245/12-827-make-business-your-business-report-on-start-ups.pdf Accessed 10.04.21.

Appendix
The Bolton Committee membership

Chair

Mr. John Bolton, DSC

Members

Mr. E.L.G Robbins, OBE
Professor J.H.B Tew, PhD
Mr. L.V.D. Tindale, CBE

Secretariat

Mr. D.C. Hartridge (Secretary) and colleagues

Research Unit

Mr. G. Bannock (Research Director) and colleagues

(after Bolton, 1971)

Index